Wounds Into Scars

Turning your sin wounds into spiritual scars

by Steve Ridgell

ISBN: 978-0-890-98938-8

Nashville, TN 37215

Cover design by Stephen Jacobs

Table of Contents

Dedication and Acknowledgements

Thank You, God, for Your mercy, grace, and patience. Thank You, Jesus, for loving me so much that You would die for me.

You cannot write a book like this, especially like this, without a wife who loves Jesus, loves you, and loves people. She has modeled grace and mercy. She has been my partner in living this Jesus life, and I am better because of her, so thank you, Marsha. I love you.

Thanks to my kids and grands. They inspire me to keep chasing Jesus. I am proud that my people are faith fighters. They are more than I could ever have imagined.

I owe an enormous debt of gratitude to the brothers in Christ who have walked alongside me. Some of their stories are in this book. Some are not. You know who you are. We have been to war together. Sometimes for each other, often for others. Thank you.

Thanks to the couples that have done life with us. You have been real church.

Special thanks to Bill and Patty Brant. They have edited, proofed, and read every book I have written, including this one. They have been more than helpers. They are friends. As is Stephen Jacobs who designed the cover. ■

Introduction

Write about what you know. That's what they say. So I suppose it was inevitable that someday I would write a book about sin. And a book about following Jesus. A book about Jesus followers who struggle with sin. Jesus followers who do not want to be unfaithful to their calling as Christians. Followers who love Jesus... yet struggle with temptation. Believers addicted to sin. Christians who sin and repent... and sin again.

I know what it is to love Jesus and battle sin. I have felt the damage to my relationship with Jesus. I have seen the damage my sin inflicted on others. I know the pain of wounds that seem too deep to heal.

But I also know the healing power of forgiveness and restoration. I have seen my wounds become scars.

So how do you write an introduction to a book about sin? Well, I am going to start by telling you the story of...

The Hole in My Head

I don't have a hole in my head now, but I did. It started because my wife saw a spot on my back that looked suspicious, so she immediately made an appointment with my dermatologist. Since I had a melanoma cut off my chest roughly 10 years earlier, she is diligent about watching for anything that doesn't look right. Turned out the spot on my back was fine, but there was one on my head that my doctor wanted to biopsy. It was a fairly large melanoma and needed a particular type of surgery—one that was not done in the West Texas town where I live, so I went to Dallas for surgery.

They excised the cancer and performed reconstructive surgery around it. It was painful, bloody, and ugly. With 60 stitches, I looked like I had lost a fight with a chainsaw. By the time they bandaged me, I looked like a mummy emerging from his tomb. It was still ugly when the bandages came off. By the time the stitches were removed, it looked better. Pretty soon, there will just be a faint scar there, but the cancer will not be. It is gone.

Obviously as a believer, I credit God for the healing. My wife took care of me. My girls are both nurses and had lots of advice. Friends brought meals, sent lots of cards, and offered more prayers than I will ever know. God used skilled surgeons and medicine. I do not want cancer to come back, so there will be lots of checking for spots that look different. I'll have regular six-month checkups. I wear hats and use lots of sunscreen. If anything does look suspicious, I'll ask my dematologist to burn it off.

So What Does All This Have to Do with Sin?

Untreated melanoma will eventually kill you. So will untreated sin. Cut it out! It is painful, ugly, and hard to do. Just like surgery. It is spiritual surgery. Get help. Have people who will be with you through the hard times. Deal with the aftermath, and be careful in the future. Take precautions, be smart, and be vigilant. Cut out anything that should not be there before it gets worse.

And know that your sin wound will someday be a faint scar.

How Can I Be So Sure?

I know because I have lived it. As long as I can remember, I have loved Jesus. Followed Him, talked about Him, and lived my life in

Him and for Him. But I also struggled. I struggled to keep sin out of my life. It was a battle. Sometimes I lost the fight. Sometimes I won. Temptation, struggle, and sin were always there. Over and over and over. Every time I fell, I was genuinely sorry. I would vow to do better, and I would do better. Until I didn't. And then I would go through the whole cycle again.

I knew the problem. I knew my weakness. And hated it. Sometimes, I even hated myself. I certainly hated what I did. Some of you reading this may even know my story. Others may know parts of it or have heard pieces of my story. Maybe you have heard me talk about it, but you are not going to hear about it here. Well, at least I won't share the details here. You will, however, learn lots about the journey. The journey is what matters, not so much the twists and turns along the way.

I always knew what the problem was. Just like most of you know your real sin battle. It is not identifying the temptation/struggle/addiction. It is defeating it. Like my melanoma.

And We Cut It Out

That is what we did with the cancer. And that is what I did with the sin. It finally came to a crisis point. I quit full-time ministry to work on it. I went back and re-dug my spiritual foundations. I connected with a therapist who also happened to be an elder and who gave a lot of helpful advice. It was advice framed by my relationship with Jesus. My wife believed I really loved Jesus, really loved her, and really wanted to be the man Jesus was calling me to be. She walked the whole journey with me. I had a band of brothers who committed to help me, to hold me accountable, and to keep pointing me to Jesus.

Then We Repaired the Damage

It's been a long time now. My wife is still beside me. I still have a band of brothers I do life with, and God has done amazing things in my life. I have been part of some amazing ministries, preached for the Herald of Truth (an evangelistic nonprofit) for over 15 years, and served as an elder in a local church for almost 15 years. Only God can write a restoration plan like that. So I will tell you what I have told hundreds of struggling Christians. I know what the wounds of sin look like. Even more, I know what it looks like when your wounds stop bleeding and turn into scars.

My wife, Marsha, and I have walked with a lot of people through a lot of crisis situations. These were people who loved Jesus, or thought they loved Him, or wanted to love Him. People who blew their life up, or who were addicted to sin, or who had a secret sin they never wanted anyone to know about. Christians who reached their crisis point and decided to confess, or were caught in their sin, or confronted by someone that knew about their sin.

Desperate believers showed up on our doorstep or blurted it out in the church foyer. Christians we met with in our living room, or in a coffee shop, or in prison.

Jesus followers who needed to get up after their fall or climb out of the ditch. We have waded into the mess of lives wounded by sin. Into the blood and the filth.

Because I've been there and got out. Sometimes the message is just to say...

"Here is your living proof that God can fix this. Can fix you. He fixed us. He fixed me."

Wounds into scars.

So What Exactly Is This Book?

This book is a collection of Scriptures, stories from the Bible, stories from my life, and some from my friends' lives. It is full of practical lessons to help Christians deeply wounded by their sin to receive grace and to live in forgiveness. To help believers in the war against Satan to recognize their sin issue, to cut it out from their lives, and then to heal the wounds.

This book is not a comprehensive theological treatise on sin. It is a practical book for those who want things to be different. It is not to take the place of therapy. There is a place for professional help, but there is also a place for spiritual counseling. This book is not a step-by-step formula for stopping sin. It is more of a compilation of practical things I have learned over the years from changing myself and helping countless others overcome their sin struggles.

Who Should Read This Book?

This book is for you if you have blown up your life with sin. Or if you are hiding a sin cancer deep in your soul, or if you find yourself caught in a cycle of fall, get up, fall, get up... and you desperately want to break that cycle. So you can watch your sin wounds become scars that reflect the healing you have experienced. So you can help others do it, too.

It is for those whose sin is public knowledge and for those whose sin no one else knows about. It's a book for those fighting for their faith and determined to win the battle.

Basically, this book is for anyone who wants answers to the questions below or for anyone who knows someone asking questions like these when examining their life and faith:

- *Is this wrong?*
- *Does it matter?*
- *Did I really do it?*
- *Am I sorry?*
- *Am I forgiven?*
- *What if others don't forgive me?*
- *Have I gotten away with it?*
- *How do I keep from doing it again?*

- *Can I ever be used again by God?*
- *What happens if I don't stop doing it?*

A Special Word to the Helpers

We are all sinners, so I do think there are great reminders here for us all as we try to be like Jesus. Many of us have defeated our demons. We have seen wounds turned into scars. We want to help others do the same.

So this book may be helpful for...

You. If you are an elder, elder's wife, minister, parent, friend of someone struggling to get past their sin. It is for Christians who want to do life in community. It's for those doing life in the hard times, being there for the brother or sister in trouble. You will find resources to offer real help when someone you love is in a fight for spiritual survival.

This is a book for anyone that knows someone asking questions like these when examining their life and faith. It is for the Christian committed to helping the struggler find answers. And to help them act on those answers.

Because there are times when all of us need help.

And times when we are the helper.

A Final Word Of Encouragement

The things I share over the following pages matter. They work. Lives can change. The demons of sin really can be defeated.

Wounds of sin become scars where healing happened.

I know because I am living proof. ■

The Real Problem with Sin

For most Christians, the issue is not that they do not know what sin is. It is not convincing them to sin less. It is not a matter of deciding to try harder or to be more concerned about the sin in their life. Sometimes, however, that is the advice you receive—advice that never gets down to the real issue, advice that misses the real point.

Fundamentally, our sin struggle is not a matter of identifying which actions—or non-actions—are wrong. The real issue is the war between God and Satan for our hearts. The basic decision is not what we are going to do, but who we are going to follow:

> 42 Jesus said to them, "If God were your Father, you would love me, for I came from God and I am here. I came not of my own accord, but he sent me.
> 43 Why do you not understand what I say? It is because you cannot bear to hear my word. 44 You are of your father the devil, and your will is to do your father's desires. He was a murderer from the beginning, and does not stand in the truth, because there is no truth in him. When he lies, he speaks out of his own character, for he is a liar and the father of lies (John 8:42-44).

You have to choose your family, and you only get one father. God wants to be your Father, and you made the commitment to be His child. Therefore, do not follow the devil as if he were your father. You will do the will of the Father you follow. Children want to please their Father.

God loves you so much that He sent Jesus to die for your sins. You believed it and by faith chose to follow Jesus. Jesus claims to be the truth. You can read that bold statement in John 14:6. And many times, Jesus uses the phrase "I tell you the truth... "

One of the truths Jesus tells you is about Satan. There is no truth in Satan. Lying is his native language—his heart language. He is a liar and the father of lies. Satan will lie about God and Jesus, he will lie about you, and he will lie about others.

Here are just a few of the lies the devil wants you to believe.

- *Everyone knows how bad you really are.*
- *You can never be forgiven.*
- *Your past defines your identity.*
- *No one really changes who they are.*
- *Shame, shame, shame... forever shame.*
- *You are a forever failure.*
- *No one knows what you are doing.*
- *You can never get past your past.*

And on and on go the lies of Satan.

So in many ways, your sin is mostly a battle about family loyalty.

You need to decide anew who really is your Father. If it is God that you truly believe and want to please, then keep reading as we look a little deeper into how sin and Satan are trying to destroy you.

A Word to the Helpers

It might be helpful to remind you what bad advice sounds like.

- *"You know this is wrong, so just stop it."*
- *"Don't you love God, your family, your church, your life, etc. . . . "*
- *"If you would just work at it, . . . "*

Trust me on this. Faithful Christians who struggle know right from wrong, they do love, and they have tried to work at it.

If we aren't careful, this kind of advice, no matter how well-intentioned, may just add to their guilt and shame. It may even cause them to feel hopeless and helpless.

Your heart is in the right place. But let's focus on the real problem, so we truly can help. ■

CHAPTER ONE

Know The Enemy's Battle Plan

You are a soldier in the Lord's army. And soldiers fight battles to win wars. God vs. Satan. Jesus vs. the powers of darkness. Truth vs. lies. God wants you to live forever with Him. Satan wants you to spend eternity away from the presence of God. You made the choice to be on the side of the Lord God Almighty, but every day you are faced with decisions that relate to that choice. Ultimately, every decision comes down to a question of the heart. It is not just about *what* you do; it is also about *why* you do what you do.

We All Live Our Love

Your life actions reflect your heart. So let's spell it out. Resisting sin is a love choice. Sinning is a love choice. You will live your love:

> [15] Do not love the world or the things in the world. If anyone loves the world, the love of the Father is not in him. [16] For all that is in the world—the desires of the flesh and the desires of the eyes and pride of life—is not from the Father but is from the world. [17] And the world is passing away along with its desires, but whoever does the will of God abides forever (1 John 2:15-17).

Do not love the things of this world. You cannot love the world and love God. Understand that your sin struggle is not simply deciding what to do—or not do. It is about remembering your true love. Jesus talked about this same idea in His Sermon on the Mount when He said that no one—that means you and me—can serve two masters (Matthew 6:24). You will end up loving one and hating the other. Committed to one while despising the other. You have to make a decision. Defeating your sin begins with deciding who you truly love. Well-meaning people used to tell me to make better choices. They were talking about behavior. Of course, that was right, but it was missing the main point. My behavior was not the choice I had to be reminded of—it was the heart choice.

God even identifies the things of the world, and they are not actions. They are the desires that lead to actions. These things of the world are not the things of the Father. The question you must constantly answer is what do you really want? For what do you hunger?

The world is driven by the desires of the flesh. Things that feel good to the point that they become a consuming hunger. When you want to satisfy an appetite so badly that you will do whatever it takes no matter the cost. When that desire becomes the driving force in your life. Even for things that are not wrong in and of themselves... like sex.

God made sex, and He made us to enjoy sex. He gives sex meaning through marriage and even expects us to enjoy it in that context—until we let the hunger for sex become greater than the drive to live in God's will. When the hunger lust for sex becomes the focus and the hunger for God takes a backseat, then we have gotten our love priorities confused.

Of course, it is not just sex. It might be alcohol, food, or any appetite that controls us instead of being controlled. The lust leads one to lose control, to hurt others, and to betray God.

Of course, everyone does not struggle that badly with physical appetites. For some, it is the desire to possess those things you see. The trap of wanting it all. The lie that you deserve the things you want. Treating wants as needs. The hunger to have what you want at all costs. Stealing, wanting what belongs to someone else. Fraud and cheating. Using others to get what you want. Loving money so much that you end up forgetting your real love. Putting money in the wrong place in your heart. Letting the hunger for owning and having lead you into evil and sin. By the way, that thought is not original with me. It is from 1 Timothy 6:10. Jesus even talked about the impossibility of serving two masters. You love and serve God. Or you love and serve money. Not both. It is interesting that right before Jesus said this in the Sermon on the Mount, He talked about making sure your eyes were clear and focused. Keep your focus where it needs to be.

Hunger for physical things and craving for material things. That is of the world, not God. But there is one more area that will lead you into addictive sin. Pride of life. Ego. The worldview that says everything is about me. I am the center of the universe, and it all revolves around me. We have all known people like that. If we are not careful, we can all be people like that. It is the idea that you are the god of your life. You are more important than anything or anyone around you. People become objects to fulfill what you want.

Sin is to love the wrong gods. Craving what the flesh wants, lusting for money, or making it all about you.

But this world and the things of this world are passing away. They will not last, and neither will these desires. Nor will what these desires lead to.

Sin is to choose oneself over God.

So do God's will, not yours. And know you will live forever.

Foy Knew It Was a War

Love God more than you love your demons. Got it! If only it were that easy in practice. You are reading this book because you know it is not that easy. We are at war against the devil and the desires of this world. And if it were easy, none of us or our people would have so much trouble with sin.

I know. I know what it is to fervently commit to not giving in to your temptations and to promise it again and again. You know it, too. Satan will not leave us alone just because we repent or just because we win one battle.

I am reminded about something Dan, one of my elder buddies, used to say to people struggling. He would talk about when he decided to quit smoking because he thought that was not something a Jesus follower should do. When I first heard him tell this, he had not smoked in over 40 years. He would talk about people who had asked God to deliver them from smoking and their testimony that God removed all desire for tobacco immediately. But it wasn't that way for Dan. After all that time, he still sometimes woke up with an intense desire to grab a cigarette. A desire he had to fight.

I always appreciated an elder telling a story like that. Sometimes the craving may absolutely go away forever. But sometimes it is a constant battle to keep your heart focused. It is not as easy as trying harder, loving God more, and knowing the right thing to do. It is always easier for me to wonder about your willpower when your struggle is not the same as my struggle. We all have our battles to fight.

My friend, Foy, got it. I don't remember the first time we met. After all, we started out together in the nursery at the church where his dad preached and where my family went. As we grew up, it was clear that everyone liked him. Even loved him. He was a gifted song leader and since I always wanted to be a preacher, we did a lot of devotionals, youth rallies, and worship assemblies together. I preached, and Foy sang.

Foy was a struggler. I always knew he loved Jesus. I always knew he was at war with the devil. He wanted to follow Jesus and would do active ministry from time-to-time. But life was hard. The desires of the flesh wage war against the desires of the Spirit.

He came to church with us once, and we sat together and sang praises together. I got pretty emotional and told him that it was like it had been 40 years earlier. He told me that sometimes he lost his song but he would not quit trying to sing it. We had lots of long talks about following Jesus, about falling, and about getting back up.

It finally caught up with Foy, and his body gave out at about 60 years old. I was out of the country preaching but wrote a eulogy that was read at his memorial. I talked about how Foy was finally at peace and that his demons were vanquished forever.

Because Foy never gave up, he kept getting back up and engaging the enemy. It was a battle and a struggle, but he never surrendered.

So I get that it is hard to stay focused. It was for Foy, and it was for me for a long time. Sometimes it still is. Maybe you get it.

Just like one of my heroes.

David: Sin, Faith, Love, and Repentance

David was the King of Israel. He was king because God does not look at the outward appearance, but He looks at the heart, and David was a man after God's own heart. The Spirit of the Lord had come upon him with power when Samuel anointed him to be king. His faith was demonstrated when he killed the lion and the bear as he protected his flocks. It was seen in the defeat of Goliath. David loved God, loved His people, and lived out his faith in amazing ways. Just read 1 Samuel 16 and 17.

He was also involved in what is one of the most famous sin events in the whole Bible. The story is in 2 Samuel 11, and it is about David, the devil, and a beautiful woman named Bathsheba. It's a story about how the devil works, about sin, and about forgiveness. So if you want to know how Satan works to destroy us, then the story of David and Bathsheba is the blueprint.

What Exactly Happened?

Kings typically went to war in the spring. But David didn't go. He sent Joab to lead the army in battle. David was not where he was supposed to be, and he was not doing what he was supposed to be doing, which made him vulnerable. It works that way in your life, too. David woke up one evening, and... wait a minute. Was the king napping or could he simply not sleep? Was he restless? Was he filled with guilt because he wasn't doing what he should have been doing or was he just bored? He took a walk on the roof. Was he looking around or checking out what—or who—might be available?

He saw Bathsheba bathing. Why was he looking? Why was she bathing in plain sight? David did a little checking, found out who she was. There it was. Another step on the wrong road. He might have argued he wasn't doing anything... yet. If only he had stopped then.

But someone (and I love this unnamed servant) pointed out she was a wife and a daughter, reminding David and giving him another way out. David, though, ignored this warning, too.

Bathsheba's husband, Uriah, was at war. Was she lonely? Depressed? Frustrated? Did she know David could see her from his rooftop? Plausible deniability. Did she see him looking?

Two vulnerable people. He may have been looking where he shouldn't have. She may have been bathing where she shouldn't have. This is how Satan works. Vulnerable people in a dangerous situation who take one step at a time down the wrong road.

Where Did It All Go Wrong?

David sent messengers to bring her to him. She went to him, and they slept together. David let the hunger in his body lead him the wrong way. Maybe Bathsheba was blinded by the wealth and power of the king, seeing the things she didn't have, seeing a way to get them. Desires of the flesh and of the eyes. The things of the world. The same temptations Satan still uses.

So why did she go? Maybe she thought she had no choice. After all, who says *no* to the king? What might have happened to her if she refused? Would Uriah have understood? Would God excuse it because she thought she had no choice? Except this king is David who was famous for the victories that God had given him. He was the king who did what was just and right for his people. What would have happened if she had said *no*? Would David have come to his senses? But she didn't say *no*.

They had sex, she went home, and no one knew. The servants sure weren't going to say anything. Uriah wouldn't have to know. Except, of course, she knew, David knew, and God knew.

Later, she realized she was pregnant. Sin has consequences. Did neither of them even consider that? But of course, you know the answer. So do I. Satan never wants you to think about consequences. He's the father of lies. *You won't get caught. No one will know. It will be like it never happened.* But you do know. And God knows.

How Can We Fix This?

Lust of the flesh. Lust of the eyes. Pride of life. That last one may have had the most extreme consequences. David thought he could fix it. Thought he could play God. He brought Uriah home to report on the battle. Brilliant. When Bathsheba turned up pregnant, everyone would assume it happened when Uriah came home. Except Uriah would not go home. Not even when David told him to visit his wife. He slept at the palace.

When David asked him why, Uriah spoke of loyalty to his men. He would not go sleep with his wife when his men were at war. So Uriah was an honorable man? Maybe a great soldier. And maybe a bad husband. Was he putting his career before his wife? Were his men more important than Bathsheba? How did she react to this? Was this a marriage in trouble? Was Bathsheba more vulnerable than anyone knew?

David even tried getting Uriah drunk, assuming surely he would go to his wife then. But no. Did David really think covering it up would make everything OK? Did Bathsheba? As if hiding it would make it like it never happened. Were David and/or Bathsheba panicked? Scared? Calculating?

Somehow David decided there was only one thing left to do. He had Joab, his trusted commander, put Uriah in the front of the battle, a dangerous place to be. It's even more dangerous when everyone withdraws and leaves you exposed to the enemy. Uriah was killed. David even tries to reassure Joab not to be upset because soldiers die in battle. Did he even hear himself? Was making Bathsheba a widow so he could marry her going to make everything right? David was involving others in his sin.

Did It Work?

We have all been there. Lying, getting others involved in covering up our sin. Pretending it is all fine if it is hidden well enough. Except you can't hide it from yourself, and you can't hide it from God.

So Bathsheba mourned her husband. Was this just a formality, or was it real? Maybe she did believe in God and found herself in a place she never expected to be. She married David and gave birth to their baby son.

But what David had done displeased the Lord. I do not think Bathsheba is absolved from her part in this, nor Joab. But David was the king. He was the man after God's own heart.

Adultery, abuse, seduction, drunkenness, murder. Involving others in sin to hide your guilt. Making it worse and worse.

So here are a few things to learn and remember from the man of God and sin.

Lessons Learned

Situations are not excuses. Consequences happen. He should have seen it coming. He should have stopped it.

Satan schemed it up. David listened to his lies. You know the lies: no harm in looking; just gathering info, you are not doing anything; you can cover this up so no one knows; you can fix this.

We've all listened to these same lies.

Uncontrolled appetites. Hungry eyes. Out-of-control ego.

And God is displeased.

The Devil Still Works the Same Way

No Christian just wakes up one morning and decides that this will be the day they ruin their life. So how does it happen? How does Satan take a man after God's own heart and lead him to make such a mess of things? How does Satan do it in your life? And more to the point, how is Satan going to come after you again?

> [13] Let no one say when he is tempted, "I am being tempted by God," for God cannot be tempted with evil, and he himself tempts no one. [14] But each person is tempted when he is lured and enticed by his own desire. [15] Then desire when it has conceived gives birth to sin, and sin when it is fully grown brings forth death (James 1:13-15).

Let's understand one important thing first. Your temptations do not come from God. Temptation is—and always will be—designed to cause rebellion against God. God does test us, but He does not tempt us. God has nothing to do with your sin. He can't. You know, that whole holy thing God has. He is holy. Sin is not. So God and sin are incompatible.

Here's how Satan tempts you. You'll be lured and enticed by your own desires. You'd better know your weaknesses/desires, because Satan sure does. I know there are things in this world that I do not want. They just have no appeal to me. But there are things of which I do have to be aware and watch out for. Different desires do not make us any better—or any worse—than someone with different desires. But you'd better know the battlefield.

Satan will try to lure you down a road that looks and feels good. It will be enticing. And it leads you away from God. David knows it, he lived it. Bathsheba in a tub. Making a connection. Asking to meet. Seeing her in person. Bathsheba was not ugly or undesirable. If she had been, she would not have been a temptation. And David was famous, the king, handsome, talented, and caring. Tempting.

If you want to do better, know your weakness, because Satan does. And he will not show up wearing a red suit and carrying a pitchfork. His horns will not be showing. Think of it this way. If chocolate pie is your weakness, Satan will not put cake in front of you. He will not use coconut pie. But you will see ads for chocolate pie. And there will be one in the bakery window. It might even be on sale.

Know your weakness. Stop following the wrong road.

Because eventually desire conceives sin. You will act on your desires. You will sin. My friend, Foy, always wanted to do better but he had a hard time changing his environment. Doing many of the same things but wanting different results. Hanging out in the bakery does not help you refuse pie. You get the point. Stop feeding your desire. It will just keep growing. If you never stop feeding your desire, it will grow up and lead you to death.

So What Now?

You are going to continue reading stories, examples, information, and encouragement to get off the wrong road and stay on the right road.

The world will continue to lure you to feed your hunger, go for the things you want, and be the god of your life.

Satan will work on your weakness. He wants you to nourish and cultivate that weakness until you end up somewhere you never intended to be.

In the story of David and Bathsheba, you saw Satan's blueprint for our destruction.

And I know it is hard. I know it, and so did Foy.

Satan and sin.

God and faithfulness.

It is a choice.

A Word to the Helpers

These are fundamental concepts to understand the struggle to overcome sin. Leaders have to share these and teach these. But I would also caution preachers and elders that we are not immune to these things of the world. You will read this several times in this book, but helpers have to stay on guard also. Many of you are "recovering sinners," so be careful.

Satan attacks leaders in the same areas as any other Christ follower.

To quote my good friend, Tim Archer: *Church leaders should be careful of girls, gold, and glory.*

Your hunger, your greed, your ego.

Be careful out there. ■

CHAPTER TWO

The Enemy Is Close So Pay Attention

You may have heard the story about the two guys walking through the jungle when they heard a lion roar nearby. Immediately, one of them started lacing up his running shoes.

"Don't be stupid. You can't outrun a lion!"

"I don't have to outrun a lion; I just have to outrun you."

It's a funny joke until you realize that is exactly how some of us think about the devil, temptation, and sin.

"At least what I did is not as bad as... "

Or, "It could have been worse."

"At least I didn't get caught."

But here is the thing about Satan. One is not enough. His job is not to catch one of us. Or just to get us one time. Sin is not measured on a sliding scale. David's sin with Bathsheba does not make our sin look better by comparison.

Here is how the devil really works:

> Be sober-minded; be watchful. Your adversary the devil prowls around like a roaring lion, seeking someone to devour (1 Peter 5:8).

This is harsh language, and it's meant to be. Far too often, we want to center our discussions of sin just around what to do or what not to do. Be sure to do the do's and don't the don'ts. Never do the don'ts or don't the do's. But we know it really is deeper than that. It is a matter of the heart, and Satan wants to rip your God heart out.

The devil is not just interested in getting you to act out. Or fail to act right.

He wants to devour you as if he is a roaring lion. He wants to destroy your relationship with God. Satan is not out to embarrass you or shame you or make you feel guilty. Those may happen, but his intention is to destroy you.

That's why we are working through a book on how to resist him. How to be alert and how to defeat the enemy.

It is spiritual war, and the devil is the enemy. He takes no prisoners.

Being alert is great. But what exactly am I being alert for?

Maybe it starts with being alert to... yourself. Be self-aware. Be sober-minded.

H. A. L. T.

I was talking to someone committed to breaking their addiction pattern. He loved Jesus and was active in helping others in a number of ways. He was also frustrated because his sin pattern was repetitive. We were talking about Satan as a roaring lion and that we had to constantly be alert. Talking about knowing our weakness, being aware of when we were vulnerable. Being aware of how Satan is seeking to pounce in our weak moments.

"**HALT**." That is what he said. I was confused and wondered what I had said that made him want me to stop. But he explained that HALT was a common acronym used in counseling, especially in addiction counseling. I had never heard it, but soon realized it was a helpful way to be aware of when you were more vulnerable, more receptive to the temptations Satan presents.

HUNGRY—Counselors use this as a reminder to keep your strength up physically. I think there's a deeper application. There are times when your physical hungers are more acute—for whatever reason. Remember when David was restless. He woke up and wandered around the roof. Hungry? You know when you are letting your cravings for sex, or alcohol, or drugs, or food move into unhealthy areas. Be aware. Pray more. Talk to a spiritual friend. Call your elder or elder's wife. Be smart about where you go. Exercise. Work out some of the hunger with a walk or run. Take the edge off.

ANGRY—Be aware when you are getting angry and frustrated. Maybe life has not been fair. Maybe you have been mistreated. Sometimes your mate really does not understand you. Work is unfair. You are not fairly compensated and do more than your share. Your kids are about to drive you over the edge. You get caught when everyone else seems to get away with it. You try to help someone, yet they don't listen, they don't care, and they ignore good advice.

Sometimes we even get mad at God.

Do not feed the anger. You will begin to justify your desire to get even. Or to lash out. You can even justify your actions. Or get so mad you do not even realize what you are doing whether that's yelling or slapping. You may even justify the next step because it is "better" than what you might have done.

Exercise self-control. Watch your emotions. Be careful when you are too mad, too worried, too giddy, too sad. So do not let shame or guilt open the door to making it worse. Be aware when your self-esteem is low. Having a pity party is an open invitation to Satan. Find someone to listen. Someone to talk you down. Talk to God. Count your blessings.

LONELY—It's hard to do life alone. You've seen the suggestions to talk to someone and be around other believers. Worshiping with a spiritual family is a big deal. Communion reminds you that you aren't alone. Live in community. Accountability matters. How lonely was Bathsheba? Or even David? My friend, Foy, had his deepest struggles when he found himself away from people who loved him, especially when he moved out-of-town or stopped coming to church.

When you are lonely, it is easy to slide into the "no one cares or no one loves me" attitude. "Everyone but me has someone." Lies from Satan will seize you when you are not alert. Then Satan will send someone—the wrong someone—with a bottle, a body, an invitation to talk about someone, or a bargain. And you take another step down the wrong road.

TIRED—Life is exhausting. Fighting your demons is exhausting. Doing the right thing is exhausting. Parenting, single parenting, ministry, shepherding, marriage, work, daily chores, school, church. Life is tough. When you're tired, you become vulnerable. Being tired dulls your awareness. You make mistakes when you are tired.

I get it because I have been there. I've burned the candle at both ends, even in ministry. People constantly call and show up. I take on more and more. Finally, one day I was going home to meet a couple for some pre-marital counseling and I couldn't do it. My wife had to call and tell me to come home. I finally told my wife, Marsha, the truth. I hadn't wanted to see them.

She took charge. She took me to the doctor to be sure everything was physically fine. She encouraged me to share with some of my closest brothers what I was feeling. The two of us instituted a rule for helping people. I could help three a night. I could do three: Bible studies, counseling sessions, hospital visits, crisis. Three. Marsha started answering the phone. She made appointments and wouldn't let me say, "Come on over." Together, we kept a list of other elders and their phone numbers.

We got more intentional about taking time off. For us, that meant going out-of-town. Staying home did not lend itself to time away from everyone. It worked! As far as I am aware, not one person failed to get help when needed. I was more rested, more focused, and more present.

HALT. It works.

You Are Not the First, and You Won't Be the Last

It is so easy to fall into the trap of Satan's lies. No one has had it this bad. My life has been more unfair than anyone else. My temptations are the hardest ever.

Remember those things of the world that we cannot afford to love: physical appetites, wanting more, ego/pride. This book is full of story after story of people who wrestled with these very things. Just like you.

So . . . you aren't unique, at least not in terms of temptation and sin. You also need to know you aren't alone in facing these battles. There is a reason to hear these stories. Others have been where you are. Learn from their mistakes and their victories.

Be encouraged by this reminder from God:

> No temptation has overtaken you that is not common to man. God is faithful, and he will not let you be tempted beyond your ability, but with the temptation he will also provide the way of escape, that you may be able to endure it (1 Corinthians 10:13).

Other believers have been where you are. We know the enemy. We know how he thinks, and we know his battle plan... and we have overcome.

Our God is faithful. Remember that temptation and sin ultimately come down to a heart decision. Remember that Satan is a liar. Remember that God is faithful.

God will not let you be tempted beyond your abilities: ability to withstand, ability to trust God to deliver you. There is no such thing as "could not resist." There is always a choice to be made. God is always stronger than Satan. So resist Satan. Satan cannot make you sin against your will. He can tempt you. But that is all. And even then, he cannot tempt you in ways you cannot handle.

Because God provides a way of escape. Looking back at the struggles in my life, I can see so many times when God put an exit ramp on my sin road. Sometimes I took it. Sometimes I blew right past it. Exit ramps like that unnamed servant of David's. The one who asked about a wife and daughter. The one David ignored.

Exit ramps. The concerned mate, friend, elder who asks if you are OK. The sudden thought that you should call someone. A glimpse of someone you know from church. Exit ramps placed to get you off the wrong road. Maybe like this book.

Sometimes You Even Have to Run . . .

Joseph had a good life. Maybe too good. He was handsome, well-built, and clearly his father's favorite son. His life was so good, his brothers were jealous. Satan tempted those brothers to sin and also used them to try to start Joseph down a road of bitterness and anger. Joseph's own brothers plotted to kill him and sold him into slavery. You want to talk about how bad life is? Joseph could be part of that conversation, but God took care of him.

He worked hard, and God was with him. Even through dark times like those. He rose to a position of prominence in the house of Potiphar, one of Pharaoh's officials. Life was good... until Mrs. Potiphar noticed him and invited him to sleep with her. He was a slave; she was in a position of power. He declined her advances. And again the next day. And the next. And... well, you get the picture. It is spelled out in Genesis 39. Joseph would not even be alone with her. He took appropriate action to avoid temptation.

That is still how Satan works to tempt you to sin. Every day. Satan doesn't give up. He tries to wear you down, looking for the day you are vulnerable. And one day, Joseph was. He found himself caught in the house alone with her. She took hold of his cloak and invited him to bed. Joseph left his cloak in her hand and ran out of the house. Sometimes the way to escape temptation is to run. I have heard people say that Joseph ran because he did not want to be in the presence of such a woman. I agree, but not in the way most people think.

Joseph ran because that was the only way to get out without sinning. He left his cloak in her hand. How did it get off? Did she rip it off, or was she slipping his coat off and Joseph realized how close he was to taking her up on her offer? Either way, he ran. Sometimes, you must take the exit ramp off the road toward sin at full speed.

Of course, you remember the rest of the story. Potiphar's wife lied and accused Joseph of attempted rape. If Satan cannot get you one way, he will try another. It is still true today. You try and battle. You get off the wrong road, and someone lies about you. It's so painful. I get that, too. I did enough things in my life that were sinful and harmful, but sometimes I did the right thing. And someone lied about me. Some people believed them.

Just like they believed Potiphar's wife. Joseph ended up in jail. You do the right thing, and you still pay for the sin you did not commit, but here's the thing: God was still with Joseph. Joseph still maintained his faith. God eventually restored him, and Joseph eventually became the Prime Minister of Egypt.

God is always stronger than Satan. You may not always see the way out, but God does. Make the right choice. Live your love. Race to the way out. Be alert because Satan will try to get you again. And again. And again. Stay faithful and focused and know that God will deliver you in the end.

Just Like My Friend J.

Satan, sin, temptation, war. If there is one thing I hope you understand from these chapters on sin, it is that you and Satan are in an all-out war for your heart and soul. God will save and deliver you, but it is sometimes a long fight. My friend J. understands.

Life was hard for J. He grew up in a church family and became a Christian as a young man. His family was a place where there was some love, some faith, some hypocrisy, and some sin. J. had some physical issues that affected his hearing and made him the butt of some cruel jokes. Eventually, he chose alcohol as a way to dull the pain, so he drank. A lot. He became a full-blown alcoholic. Stopped going to church. Didn't stop believing, just lost his desire to fight.

He would tell you as an adult that he loved Jesus, Lynyrd Skynyrd, and alcohol. Over time, the love for alcohol got stronger. Eventually that love cost him his marriage, his driver's license, and even his faith, were buried by the consequences of his choices.

I met J. through Bill, a minister and an alcoholic. That is how he introduced himself. He was helping J. get back on his feet, and I was helping out by trying to get J. some work. I owned a phone book delivery service at the time and hired him. J. was smart, hardworking, honest... and an alcoholic.

We spent a lot of time on the road talking about Jesus. And my demons. And his. My wife and I helped him get his driver's license restored. Even loaned him our vehicle to take his driving test. When he passed the test, we celebrated with chocolate chip cookies my wife baked.

J. got a full-time job. Started going to Alcoholics Anonymous. Went back to church. And we had a few late-night sessions together when he slipped and fell. But even those times were different. Confession, repentance, and doing the hard work to battle his sin.

Two steps forward, one step back. Fall, get up, fall, get up. But he always got back up. He continued to fight his demons and got back in church.

It did not happen overnight. It took years of fighting, but J. made it. Today, he is a faithful Christian, happily married, even getting some treatment for his hearing issues. And he is sober.

J.'s story is the story of a faith fighter. Re-digging his faith foundations because two recovering sinners got into his life.

He worked hard, and when he fell, he kept getting back up.

Today he is still alert to the schemes of Satan.

And he is faithful.

A Word to the Helpers

I want to share a couple of reminders for the spiritual leaders who are committed to helping the battlers among us. First, watch yourself. HALT works for you, too. You get hungry also. And even with the people you are helping, you can get angry, tired, and even lonely if you are the only one trying to help, so stay alert.

I also said quite a bit to the strugglers about talking to someone, listening to spiritual advice, hanging out with their spiritual community. That means you have to be pro-active as a leader/shepherd in reaching out.

Ask about their danger times. After work? Friday nights? Payday? I had a preacher friend who admitted he was most vulnerable on Mondays. He was tired, emotionally spent, and not on his guard. When they identify the vulnerable gaps, you help fill them. Coffee after work. Game nights on Friday. Lunch on Monday. Prayer time on payday. These are also excellent opportunities to involve other helpers. They can help stand in the gaps.

You get the idea. Because Satan wants to devour us.

All of us. ■

Confession Is ~~Good~~ Essential for the Soul

1 Blessed is the one whose transgression is
forgiven, whose sin is covered.

2 Blessed is the man against whom the LORD counts
no iniquity, and in whose spirit there is no deceit.

3 For when I kept silent, my bones wasted away
through my groaning all day long.

4 For day and night your hand was heavy upon me;
my strength was dried up as by the heat of summer.

5 I acknowledged my sin to you, and I did not cover my iniquity; I said, "I will confess my transgressions to the LORD," and you forgave the iniquity of my sin (Psalm 32:1-5).

There is good news about your sin. It can be forgiven. Your sins can be covered up. God will not even count them against you. I live every day of my life in awe of this blessing. You see, I know all the bad things I have done. All the good things I did not do. I know. God knows. Mercifully, He is not counting those sins against me because I have confessed my sins and taken ownership of them.

But here is the thing about confession: It must be done without deceit. You do not get forgiveness by trying to trick, fool, deceive God. Because you can't. You are not going to pull a fast one over on God.

Remember that sin ultimately is a heart issue. So is confession. Have a true heart, a pure heart, an honest heart when talking to God about your sin.

Bad things happen when you hold it in. You deceive yourself. Do not hide your sin, because you cannot. God knows and you know, so... bad things happen when you do not deal with your sin. When you fail to acknowledge it, or face it, or own it, that failure will make it seem as if your very bones are wasting away. You may groan all day and all night. I remember being unable to sleep, tormented by my guilt. You, too, have had those nights.

If you really are a Jesus person, it will tear you up until you deal with your sin. Because God's hand is on you. Your very strength is being sapped. God intends for you to confess your sin. You will not find peace until you do.

What does God want from you when you sin? He wants you to acknowledge your sin to Him. Stop covering it up. Stop making excuses. Stop ignoring your failure. Confess your sin to God. Every sin is ultimately against God above all, not against yourself or other people or your church. First and foremost, your sin is against your God.

During my darkest times of struggle, I spent a lot of time trying to figure out how to explain/talk/confess about my sin to my wife, my kids, my church, my friends. Until I finally realized it started with my talking to God, and He forgave the guilt of my sin. That is something no one else can do. Not me or another person or a church. They may forgive the hurt or the damage, but only God can forgive the sin. Forgiving sin is God's business.

And that is where real healing has to begin.

So, remember the good news about your sin: Confess it, and God will forgive. It will not count against you. It is covered up. Forever.

A Word to the Helpers

When someone trusts you enough to confess their sins to you, it is natural to share in the relief the struggler feels that it is finally "out in the open." It is easy to slip into the conversation of how, if, or when to tell others. Do not, however, fail to help them confess to God. It is the essential first step to healing. ■

CHAPTER THREE

Do Not Stay Silent

You've recognized by now that I'm a storyteller. Stories are relatable. Jesus taught that way. It always helps you understand your situation better when you know that others have gone through the same kind of experience. As I relate these stories, it is reasonable to ask: How do the subjects of these stories feel about having their stories told?

For lots of them, this is just a continuation of what they have been doing. They tell their stories privately and publicly. Many of these stories have been shared in various ways over time with their church families. They are glad if their story helps someone else draw closer to Jesus. But still, telling/reading their story is painful for some of them. I get it. Sharing parts of my story is still painful for me. Regardless, like me, they want to help.

Some are still working through their guilt and shame. Some of these stories are true but I use different names or only initials. Occasionally I will share a story that is actually a composite of several people, because situations are similar. Many times, I have shared a story with someone only to have them say that it sounds just like what they are experiencing. That is true. Sin, temptation, the struggle to confess, repentance, restoration, and healing are themes common to all our struggles, even from the beginning of time.

So I want to share a composite story from three or four different people. They are so similar that each of them would think this is their story alone, just with a couple of details confused. It's a story that shows the importance of real and true confession and a story of how sometimes admission is not really confession at all.

Let's call them Sue and Fred.

I Maybe... Sort of Did It... Or Not

They were both active church leaders in positions of authority and ministry. They were always at worship with their families, served on many committees, and studied in small group together.

And they had an affair.

I was pulling into the parking lot, preparing to preach when someone in Sue's family called me. They'd found evidence of an affair. There was proof. With a broken heart, I met with her family.

Deny. Deny. Deny. That was the pattern when she was confronted with the evidence. Every one of the many, many calls were church-related, even the ones lasting for over an hour. The calls that were not church business were counseling. Any time they had been together, it was counseling. Maybe it started that way, but the evidence certainly pointed to a different conclusion.

Fred was different. He agreed to meet with my wife and me and another elder couple. Fred did not deny it at all. In fact, he absolutely admitted it, but didn't really confess it. There was a lot of emotional talk about what a sorry person he was. He felt terrible that he had hurt his wife. He was sorry for the mess we all faced and was sorry for the consequences. He never really confessed to sin; no talk of how much he regretted the action.

This, in turn, led Sue to decide to "confess." She would confess that it happened, but it wasn't really her fault. They each admitted that they were blinded by the physical attraction, money, attention given by the other one. Fred and Sue each talked about how the other one was everything their current mate was not. Sue admitted what happened—and was happening. She felt miserable about where her life now was. She realized this was not what God wanted for her life. And she talked a lot about how Fred loved God and loved her, and that he was really sorry for what was happening. Sue was confessing for Fred. Not for herself.

Sue was taking all the blame and was mad that we were damaging him. And who was I—directed at me personally—to confront anyone about sin because everyone knew about my past?

Fred began to reject any action we took concerning Sue. Even confronting her would keep her from ever coming back to church. We were showing no understanding or sympathy. We were purely judgmental. No love. That led to a lot of discussion from us about grace and forgiveness. And lots of discussion of our concern about the lack of repentance and confession from each of them.

Separate conversations that were quite similar. We began to realize there was way too much talk about the consequences, but not much from either of them about the sin. They wanted to focus on managing the results. We wanted to get to the real issue: sin and confession.

All of this eventually led to their removal from positions of leadership. Sue stepped down grudgingly. Fred had to be removed. He was angry. In that anger, he said harsh things said to us and about us. We listened to pleading from Sue not to remove Fred from his position of leadership and why it should not happen. People would talk. He had done so much good. Both of those were true by the way, and both of them missed the point. Fred was angry that he was being "punished" when there were lots of other sinners at our church in leadership. True. Yet it still missed the point.

He was not removed because of what he had done; he was removed because of what he was not doing. No repentance. No real confession.

Sue even asked if we were happy about all the pain and suffering we were causing in their marriages and in their lives.

We had to carefully spell out that we did not cause any of this. Their sin had led to this. We even admitted we might not be handling everything perfectly, but we were doing the best we could to lead them to real confession and repentance. But since they would not, we must do what we could to protect our flock. We had to remind each of them that there would be nothing to handle were it not for their sin.

Sue and Fred were active Christians who found themselves in a mess. Phone calls. Time together. An affair. Fred ended his marriage. Sue eventually did come to confess and repent. But it took a long time. And until she did, it almost destroyed her.

What Does Confession Sound Like?

Maybe it will be helpful to take a deeper look at what real confession looks and sounds like—and why it is so difficult to do. There are four aspects of confession that I listen for when trying to help struggling believers. These do not always occur at once. They overlap, and they often play out over some time, but these are the four elements of true confession:

I did it. Let's start with the obvious. Admit what you have done. As you saw from the previous story, sometimes people will initially deny their actions, even in the face of overwhelming evidence. Why lie? If you are a Christian committed to following Jesus, why lie about your sin? Image is one reason, especially for church leaders. Everyone cultivates an image of how you want to be perceived by others. Hopefully, the reality matches the image. What you see really is what you get. This is a hard one for parents also. For your kids to realize that Mom and Dad are not perfect is hard to face. You believe people will lose respect for you if they know what you've done. This is especially true if this a repetitive sin. These are legitimate fears, and they are true. It is also true that your courage in acknowledging your sin will earn respect. And for the parents out there: Teaching your children to repent, confess, and change is a great lesson. Of course, we all wish they did not have to learn it by our example, but it is still a great spiritual life lesson.

There is also the fear of the unknown. What happens when this is known? Fear of consequences is real. Forgiveness is guaranteed. Protection from consequences is not always assured. Will there be financial repercussions? Are there legal implications? What happens to my marriage? Or my job? Or my involvement at church?

Sometimes it's even easy to fall into the trap of revisionist history. As long as no one else knows, it didn't really happen. Of course, you know, and God knows. Ignoring it because no one has found out will eat you alive.

So take a deep breath, look in the mirror, and confess your sin. Get on your knees, and admit it to God. When someone sits in our living room and asks for help in dealing with their sin, my wife and I immediately make it clear that healing begins the moment they confess their sin.

I did it. No excuses, no blaming someone else, no cover up.

That is the when the bleeding stops, and the healing begins.

It was wrong You would think this would be automatically assumed, but there are times when someone decides to admit they did it, only to immediately justify their actions. "I did it, but it was not really wrong" is not confession. If that is true, then there is nothing to confess. If it is not wrong, it is not sin. I do have to admit that it is almost painful to watch Christians wrestle with how to excuse behavior they know is wrong.

Excuses. How can it be wrong if...

Our culture says it is OK.

Love is the most important thing, so...

Everyone/lots of people/even many Christians do it

What about so and so? They do this. Are you also talking to them?

It could have been so much worse.

Well, at least I didn't do ______________________________ .

Every one of these excuses may be true, but they all miss the point. Sin is not ultimately about culture. Or other people. Or even yourself. Sin is against God above anyone and anything else. There will always be someone—maybe in church, maybe not—that will tell you what you are doing is not really wrong. The point is to be honest with what God says about your behavior. My friends in the previous story wanted to talk about pain and hurt and reputation and love and other people. What they did not want to talk about was God.

Real confession. I did it. It is wrong.

I am sorry. Well, of course if you are ready to admit you did it and you were wrong, then you obviously are sorry. Not necessarily. I appreciate honesty and even admire it, especially in times of spiritual crisis. Over the years I have learned not to assume that being sorry automatically goes with the first two. For a long time, I thought everyone was like me. I did a lot of things that were ~~wrong~~ sinful. And I was always sorry for the sin above all else:

- *Be sorry. Not just sorry you got caught, or sorry for the consequences, or for the hurt caused.*
- *Be sorry for the sin.*
- *Acknowledge you did it.*
- *Accept that it was wrong.*
- *And regret doing it.*

But there is one more key component of confession.

I want to change. Be sorry enough to quit. Be sorry enough to change. This may be the point where confession gets the most real... and the most difficult. More than the emotion of regret, this is where confession becomes action. This is the point where you decide you do want to live as God asks—and expects—you to live. To follow Jesus. Not just work on the consequences, but work on the life.

This is hard. This is where your true heart leads to a different life.

This is where your wounds start to become scars.

Where confession leads to a different life. Where the hard work begins.

And It Is Not Easy

I still remember some of my early attempts to confess. I would cautiously, and with some fear, admit to someone that I was in a struggle. Most of the time, this confession was to people who loved me, forgave me, and wanted the best for me. I was hugged, prayed over, admonished to never do anything like that again. Then everyone left. I would resolve to do better.

I would be shocked when everything did not change right away. Or when temptation came back. It took some years before I understood that changing is not easy.

I should have read Paul more closely. Because he got it:

> [15] For I do not understand my own actions. For I do not do
> what I want, but I do the very thing I hate. [16] Now if I do what
> I do not want, I agree with the law, that it is good. [17] So now it
> is no longer I who do it, but sin that dwells within me. [18] For I
> know that nothing good dwells in me, that is, in my flesh. For I
> have the desire to do what is right, but not the ability to carry
> it out. [19] For I do not do the good I want, but the evil I do not
> want is what I keep on doing. [20] Now if I do what I do not want,
> it is no longer I who do it, but sin that dwells within me
> (Romans 7:15-20).

Verse 15 expresses the feelings of every believer who battles their sin addiction. You really do confess your sin and want to do better. Your heart is turned to God. You never want to go down the wrong road again. You know what is good and right. And that is what you want to do. You know what is wrong. That is what you do not want to do. God's law and His will are good. Following them leads you to the life you desire to live. You hate the sin you do. You may even hate yourself at times for doing it.

Then you end up doing what you hate—the very thing you never wanted to do again. Not the good you want to do, but the evil you do not want to do. Not doing what you love. Doing what you hate. Again. And again.

There are two great truths in this passage that can change everything.

You cannot do this on your own. You can't. You may want to, but you do not have the ability on your own to follow through. No matter how hard you try, no matter how hard you work at it; you must have help. Take a step back to the heart issue. It starts with loving God, and you ask Him for help. Jesus can deliver you. God provides resources to help you: the way out that God puts in your path, the Holy Spirit makes you holy, the Bible instructs you, and a community of faith will walk with you.

You cannot do this on your own. The good news is, you don't have to. Confess. Let help and healing begin.

Another great truth. Your sin does not define you. It is not who you are. Understand the difference between your identity and your action. Your identity is that you are a child of God. Satan wants to define you by your worst actions. He says you are what you have done. He is a liar. God has forgiven you in Christ. God does not count your sin against you. He does not identify you by your sin. You shouldn't either:

> [24] Wretched man that I am! Who will deliver me from this body of death? [25] Thanks be to God through Jesus Christ our Lord! (Romans 7:24-25a)

That conflict between who you are and what you sometimes do will make you miserable.

Of course it is hard because we are at war. and this is a battle. But Jesus can—and will—deliver you.

I am living proof.

So Is Paul

Paul was a great man of God who took incredible risks for the gospel. Read the last half of 2 Corinthians 11 (verses 23-33) to see the list of the things Paul endured for the sake of making Jesus known to others. He accomplished so much for the kingdom of God. In the first section of 2 Corinthians 12 you can read about an amazing vision experience Paul had in which he saw things he could not even talk about. If tradition is to be believed, Paul was martyred for his faith by being beheaded outside Rome in 57 A.D.

These are the type of things that would make it easy to think how great Paul was and perhaps even for Paul himself to think how great he was. Except that Paul was conscious not to boast of what he had done. In fact, he would only boast of his weakness. You get a sense that Paul made a point to emphasize how God does His best work with His weakest people.

This leads to the famous "thorn in the flesh" passage in 2 Corinthians 12:7-10:

> 7 So to keep me from becoming conceited because of the surpassing greatness of the revelations, a thorn was given me in the flesh, a messenger of Satan to harass me, to keep me from becoming conceited. 8 Three times I pleaded with the Lord about this, that it should leave me. 9 But he said to me, "My grace is sufficient for you, for my power is made perfect in weakness." Therefore I will boast all the more gladly of my weaknesses, so that the power of Christ may rest upon me. 10 For the sake of Christ, then, I am content with weaknesses, insults, hardships, persecutions, and calamities. For when I am weak, then I am strong (2 Corinthians 12:7-10).

If Paul had a weakness, it may have been his ego. Remember that pride is one of the things of the world we cannot love. Paul wrote about the fact that to keep his ego in check, he had been given a messenger from Satan. His thorn in the flesh. What was this thorn in the flesh? Some have argued that it was a physical weakness or condition, perhaps weak eyesight. Maybe, but Paul does not identify what it was for sure. Could it have been a spiritual weakness, a temptation where he was vulnerable? He did ask God on at least three occasions to take it away. By now you can see where this is going. How many times have you begged God to take away the temptation that plagues you? To take away some physical desire or some craving for things you do not have?

God did not remove Paul's thorn. God reminded him that His grace would be sufficient. Grace is God's forgiveness that we cannot earn and do not deserve. Did God want Paul to wrestle with his demons and overcome them? Did He want Paul to understand that it was only by grace that he could do the things he did? Was it to help him remember that the power was never from Paul but only from God?

Is that why some of us battle our demons for a long time? Learning to depend on God's grace. Realizing with Paul that God's power is made perfect in weakness. Staying alert. Being on guard. Battling the forces of evil in our own life so we would not become conceited and think the power was ours.

Boast in your weakness, so Christ's power is upon you. Because when we are weak, then we become strong. Maybe the real key to living power-filled lives for God is not the absence of struggle and temptation. It may be that overcoming those temptations unleashes the power of God in our lives. Because Jesus—and only Jesus—has the power to change lives forever.

Let me be clear.

I am a sinner. A forgiven sinner. I am keenly aware of my

weakness, my battles. I am totally dependent upon God. Dependent on His love, His mercy, and His grace.

That is my story.

It's the story of how God took a beaten, battered soul that still believed in His Son and wanted to serve Him desperately.

The blood from the wounds of my sin was flowing, and God stopped the bleeding, healed the wounds. Because of His mercy and grace, I have forgiveness and restoration.

Till the wound became nothing more than a scar.

My desire is to help others learn the same lesson—turning wounds into scars.

This is my story.

A Word to the Helpers

When having to confront someone with the fact that their sin is known, it is wise to have someone else involved, partly to be sure there are numerous ears to hear the discussion but also, to show that support is there. They must know that they are loved,and we are there to help. If possible, we let the people in trouble tell us the people with whom they feel close and want to help on this journey. Then we utilize them to help.

I also need to point out one mistake I often made in the early years of my spiritual counseling. I believed that someone admitting sin was the same as their being sorry for the sin. Sometimes there was genuine sorrow, but the sorrow was for getting caught or for the consequences. I have learned to listen for, "sorry I sinned," not just "I'm sorry." There is a difference.

When strugglers are making those confession statements, it is helpful to remember that these statements obviously build on one another. That is why they sometimes occur over days, weeks, or even months.

Be patient. ■

CHAPTER FOUR

Own Your Story

Confession is the beginning. It is the start of a different life, one empowered by your admitting to God that you are still a sinner and that you cannot overcome it on your own. Confession is to realize and admit that you cannot obtain forgiveness on your own and that you are indeed powerless to live the life you want. That's where Jesus comes in. Your story, like my story, is that of a believer who struggles to get past—and over—the sin in our lives.

Confession is to own your story. All of it. The faith, the sin, and the struggle. It is hard to admit your own weakness and failure. Confession requires honesty, vulnerability, and transparency. It means facing your guilt and shame.

It's also the first step you take to recovery, forgiveness, and living the life you desire.

It means having a heart for God—and admitting it.

Which leads us back to the story of David.

I Am the Man

Let's revisit the story of David. Talk about a mess. Distracted, off mission, and vulnerable. Bathsheba, lonely and vulnerable. Satan, hungry to devour someone. Sin. Adultery. Murder. Consequences. Shattered faith. Cover-up. Nothing as it should be. And yet... deep in the depths of his soul, David still believes. However, he is clearly in trouble and in need of focus and direction.

In the middle of all this mess, God sent a man named Nathan to talk to David.

This is the part of the story where two heroes meet. David is my hero and always has been. I loved the Goliath story when I was growing up, and I love this story. This is the part of the book where some might say, "Well, of course you do."

"It is the story of someone who really messed up their life. And since you messed up your life and since you know a lot of people who have messed up their lives, then of course, he is your hero."

I do love David because I see so much of myself in his story. Not the sin part. It is what happens after that makes him my hero. Part two of this story is what I want to emulate.

The other hero is Nathan. God's man is in trouble, so God sends another of His men to help him. For those of you in a mess, God is sending someone to you. Watch for them. Listen to them.

Nathan went to see David. I can only imagine what he must have thought. He was going to confront the king, the national hero, about his sin. Nathan told David a story. Maybe that is why I like Nathan so much. Maybe that is one reason I like to use stories so much.

What Did Nathan Say to David?

Nathan told David there was a rich man with lots of livestock and a poor man with one little lamb that he treated as one of the family. The rich man was throwing a banquet for someone visiting him, and he took the poor man's pet lamb to be the meal. David was furious when he heard the story. He said the offender should die and pay back at least four times the cost of the lamb.

That reaction is why I know that David was still a man of faith. He still clearly knew right from wrong and desired that right be done. He hated evil and felt pain and righteous anger at the evil done. He just did not see himself in the story.

That really hits home, doesn't it? I can see the evil in others so much quicker than I see it in myself sometimes. You know, the whole speck in your eye, log in my eye that Jesus talked about in the Sermon on the Mount.

That's how someone who loves Jesus can get in one mess after another. We tend to look out the window instead of in the mirror. Sometimes we all need someone to connect the dots for us, which is why Nathan had to tell David...

"You are the man."

David heard Nathan.

"I have sinned against the Lord."

That is a statement of faith. That is why David is my hero. He is a faith fighter. He doesn't give up. He owns his sin. He moves from "You are the man" to "I am the man."

Both of these heroes, Nathan and David, were faith fighters. In this story, both were fighting for David's faith. Both realized the main issue: David's heart and David's relationship with God. David got it right; he sinned against the Lord. The main issue was not Bathsheba. Or Uriah. Or Joab. The main issue was God.

David confessed that he did it, and it was wrong.

What About the Consequences?

Let's start with the most important result of confession: The Lord has taken away your sin, and you will not die. The best news in this story is that God forgives. We must declare this good news to the sinner. God takes away sin. You will not die. This is where the healing began for David and where healing still begins today.

I did it, and it was wrong.

You are forgiven, and you will not die.

But there were two consequences.

The enemies of the Lord will show utter contempt. When one of God's people sins, we negate so much of the good news message. In Christ there is forgiveness. Yes, but as Christians, we are being made new in the image of Christ.

We are His disciples, His followers. He gives life. When we sin, we negate so much of that message. We are supposed to be the living witness to the power of the gospel, and the enemies of the Lord look on us with contempt when we are such poor witnesses. Can't a believer sin, confess, repent, and still be powerful witness to the Lord?

Of course, but that happens over time, and it is powerful. I would suggest that I am living proof of that, but initially, our sin reflects badly on God.

Secondly, the child will die. God spared David the punishment by forgiving his sin, but there was a consequence. Sometimes the consequences are hard. They may seem unbearable.

In David's case, it is how the consequence played out that showed David's faith. He fasted and prayed, thinking and hoping and believing that God might spare his son. He asked God to manage the consequence differently, pleading for it not to be as bad. Then David noticed the servants whispering together and he realized the baby had died. God did not answer the prayer the way David wanted, but David did not blame God. After all, he understood who caused all this. He had.

David got up, cleaned himself up, and asked for food. His servants thought this behavior might have been backward: praying and fasting while the child was alive, yet cleaning up and eating after the death.

Here are the two great lessons for managing consequences from my hero, David.

Get on with life. It may take time, but life does not end because your sin has consequences. It may be different in ways you never dreamed, but God is not through with you.

Know where you are going. David told the servants that he knew his son would never come to him. He was dead. He also told them he could go to his son. Hope of heaven is powerful. No matter the consequences, sin is forgiven. That means you will live with God forever. No matter what.

You can ask God to manage consequences, even to spare you from some of the consequences. I have done that over my sin and often over the sin of others. Sometimes God answered those prayers as asked. Sometimes He did not. But He is God, and life in Christ will go on. Be faithful. No one can take away the hope of heaven because you are forgiven.

Believers sin and confess. God forgives and restores.

Our Sin and God's Promise

God has always known His people would be torn between faith and sin, and that these two things are not mutually exclusive. So, for all the faithful strugglers reading this, let me share with you my "go-to" passage for struggling sinners:

> 5 This is the message we have heard from him and proclaim to
> you, that God is light, and in him is no darkness at all. 6 If we
> say we have fellowship with him while we walk in darkness, we
> lie and do not practice the truth. 7 But if we walk in the light,
> as he is in the light, we have fellowship with one another, and
> the blood of Jesus his Son cleanses us from all sin. 8 If we say we
> have no sin, we deceive ourselves, and the truth is not in us. 9 If
> we confess our sins, he is faithful and just to forgive us our sins
> and to cleanse us from all unrighteousness. 10 If we say we have
> not sinned, we make him a liar, and his word is not in us
> (1 John 1:5-10).

God is light, and there is no darkness at all in Him. If you claim fellowship with God—and we strugglers do—then you cannot walk in the darkness. If you believe it is acceptable to live outside the light, you are lying to yourself and others. You are not living by the truth. Christians cannot stay in the darkness and be true to their faith.

Darkness always exists just outside of the light, and shadows are the in-between land. Do not live in the shadows trying to hold on to both worlds. Living in the shadow-land makes it too easy to slip into the darkness. Once there, it's easy to stay there. It is also possible to live in the shadows and occasionally slip into the light so you end up fooling yourself about where you really are walking. Center your walk directly in the light.

Jesus is the light center. Jesus is the light center because He is the light of the world. Walking with Jesus in His light is the basis of our fellowship with Jesus and with one another. We are on a common journey. Our hearts, our focus, our vlives are centered on Jesus. In this light, the blood of Jesus purifies us from all sin.

So… Do Faithful Christians Sin?

Wait a minute now. If we're centered in the light, wouldn't that mean we don't sin. I grew up thinking if I just tried hard enough, I would never sin. Sin was a failure and weakness on my part. The more spiritual I became, the less I would sin. Or, the less I sinned then the more spiritual I was becoming, right?

I was confusing my heart with my actions. The focus became external, not internal. The answer to sin was to try harder. Be better. Just stop sinning. I'm not sure I was ever taught that explicitly, but during my worst sin struggles, that was the advice I received: Try harder, and just stop it.

This passage reminds us that even when we're walking in the light, we sometimes sin. Our walk has stumbles, and sometimes we even fall down. We venture out of the light. The answer to sin is not to live perfectly, it is to live in the light. Walking in the light is not to be perfect or sinless; it is to be faithful. Sin cannot survive in the light. When we walk in the light, our sin is purified/forgiven/overcome by the blood of Jesus. Center your heart on God and Jesus.

Do not, however, claim to be sinless. You're just fooling yourself and not being truthful. Here's a word to those committed to helping those caught in sin—do not act as if you never struggle with sin.

Confess your sin. Own your sin, and confess it. Be like David: I did it, and it was wrong. Confess it to God above anyone else. Confess it to those who will help you deal with it. Confess it to those who are there to help. Confess it to those with whom you walk in fellowship. Confess to those with whom you live your life, not just those you see at church. That's who will be there for you.

Confess your sin. Not just that you have sinned and not just in some vague, non-specific, generic way that really admits nothing. That does not mean you have to share every detail of your sin to others. God knows the details, and so do you. Details are not healthy for you to remember, and others do not necessarily need to know the who, what, when, where, and how.

Please remember that God is faithful. He will do what He says He will do. If he says He will not hold our sins against us when we confess, know that He is going to do exactly what He said. You can trust God to be faithful and just. He will forgive your sins, and He will cleanse you from all our unrighteousness.

Confess your sin, and walk in the light. Just don't claim not to sin. The commitment to help others in the hard times of their sin is not because we are sinless—perfect. It is because we are forgiven. Claiming to be sinless just makes God a liar and that God's Word is not needed in our lives. After all, if I can be perfect, I do not need confession or even forgiveness. I don't even need Jesus if I can be perfect.

So What Again Do We Learn from This Verse?

Get in the light of Jesus. Stay out of the shadows. We are all sinners. I am here to help not because I am perfect, but because I am forgiven. I am holy because of the blood of Jesus. You can be, too. I was wounded by my sin, but that wound is now a scar. So come back into the light. Confess your sin, and be forgiven. Be purified. Own your sin. Get on with life as a forgiven sinner.

Just Like One of My Good Friends

There are two things I absolutely know about my friend, Stephen. One is that he loves Jesus with everything he has. And two, he has struggled with his sin for most of his life. That struggle has cost him dearly. It has cost him friendships and his marriage.

I—and others—have walked beside him, counseled him, spoken truth into his life, admonished, encouraged, prayed, well . . . you get the picture. And he still battles. His demon is lust, and he fights it every day. He is working on his ninth year of sexual sobriety, and he still battles every day.

He has asked me why I haven't given up on him. If I'm completely honest, I've occasionally asked myself that same question. Why haven't I washed my hands of him? Why don't I quit on him?

Here is why.

He is a faith fighter. He never blames anyone else. He does not try to justify his sin. He confesses his failures and his temptations. He fights to do better. He never quits. He is happy about eight years sobriety and gives God the credit, but he knows the fight is not over and may never be over. But it does show he is doing better. He clings desperately to his faith. Over time, the work has moved from getting out of the darkness to now staying in the light. Faith fighting.

Stephen is not looking for the easy way out. He doesn't want someone to tell him his struggle is not so bad.

That's why he's going to make it.

I did it. It's wrong. I'm sorry. Let's get to work.

That's why I don't give up on him. I get it. Our battles may be different, but the war is the same. He doesn't have to do this alone. He needs to see that wounds do become scars.

I will not quit on him.

Neither will God.

What Good Is A Sinner Anyway?

There is an undercurrent of fear in every believing sinner, not just of guilt or what people will think or how they will treat you. There is also the worry that you have ruined your ability to make a difference for the kingdom any longer—that you're damaged goods. After all, what good is a sinner? More to the point, how can someone like you ever be part of what the sinless Jesus is doing in this world? You know you. What can you possibly have to offer Jesus? Why would He even want to use you?

You are not the first to feel this way.

My friend, Peter, felt this way, and this part of his story is told in Luke 5.

Peter was a professional fisherman, obviously good at his job. Sometimes, as in any job or any fishing trip, things don't work out as you planned. Peter and his brother, Andrew, had fished all night and caught nothing. That, of course, means no payday. They pulled the boats up on the shore and washed off their nets.

Jesus was also there. He was teaching the people, and they were crowding closer and closer. He spotted Simon Peter's boat, climbed in, and asked him to take Him out a way, so it was easier to speak to the crowd. Peter must have been tired, dirty, and frustrated from the night before, but he did what Jesus asked.

By the way, Peter was an amazing man: sleepy from working all night, sitting in a boat with the waves gently moving, and listening to a sermon. And he apparently stayed awake. Amazing.

When Jesus finished speaking, He told Peter to put out in the deep water and let down his nets for a catch. Is this a "thank-you" from Jesus? Did He want to make a point about His power? This wasn't an invitation to go fishing. This was a statement of fact about catching fish. Peter was polite and pointed out to Jesus that they had worked hard all night and did not catch anything. Was Peter politely telling Jesus there were no fish? Was he wanting to spare Jesus embarrassment? After all, there were no fish, and Jesus just said "catch" fish. Did Peter doubt what Jesus was saying? Or was Peter pondering out loud how this was going to happen?

Faith, Sin, and Catching Men

"But because you say so, I will let down the nets." This is Peter's great statement of faith. There are no fish, I am not sure how this is going to work... but because you say so... Peter's heart was turned to Jesus, it is clear who he chose to follow, and he was centered in the light of Jesus.

Even so, he was shattered by the power of God. They began to catch fish. So many fish that the nets were breaking as they hauled them in. So many fish that they piled up in the boat and started sinking. So many fish that they had to signal their partners on the shore to come help with the catch.

This is a great place in the story to talk about the power of our God or about how Jesus provides way more than we dreamed. Even more, how Jesus broke through all the conventional wisdom and ordinary trappings of life. What a time to celebrate, to worship, to give thanks!

Peter, though, didn't do any of those. He was shattered by the incredible power of Jesus. He literally fell to his knees and told

Jesus to leave him, because in his own words, "I am a sinful man."

It may happen to you. Somewhere in your sin, your struggle, or your restoration, you too will be knocked to your knees. You will be overwhelmed by the surpassing greatness and power of your God. It may be when you realize how much God has forgiven you. It may be when God acts in a way you could not see or even imagine that changes everything for you. There will be times when all you can do is fall to your knees in front of the Lord God Almighty.

And then Satan whispers, "Look at Him. Look at you. Who are you to be in the presence of sinless Jesus? You are not worthy. You will never change. You are a sinner who should never be in the presence of the Son of God."

I don't know everything Peter must have been thinking, but I do know this: Jesus did not leave him.

The Holy God and the unholy you.

Jesus, who makes a way for us to have a relationship in spite of sin.

The Jesus who will not leave you.

In fact, Jesus told Peter two things to which all of us should always cling:

> "Do not be afraid; from now on you will be catching men." (Luke 5:10b)

Stop worrying about your past or your future. Live in today. This is the day that the Lord has made. Rejoice and be glad because through Jesus, your sins are not counted against you. You are going to catch men with Jesus.

Peter, Andrew, James, and John. They pulled the boats on the shore, left everything where it was, and followed Jesus.

The unholy you who is being made holy by Jesus.

You will be used by God to catch other sinners, so they, too, can be holy by the blood of Jesus.

So they can catch other holy sinners.

Who will catch other holy sinners?

Who... well, you see where this is going as well as what God is doing.

What good is a sinner like you?

You're good enough in Jesus to be used to bring others back to God.

A Word to the Helpers

Sometimes we need someone to help us, and sometimes we are the ones God calls to help others. Perhaps you are the one God wants to send into someone's life to help them, to redeem them, to restore them.

If you're the one being sent, I know how hard it is. It isn't easy to ring the doorbell, to make the phone call. It is scary, painful, and it hurts. It requires great faith and courage to step into the mess of a broken life and help restore someone.

When reading about how Nathan approached David, we can note five things he said, which can help give us a blueprint we can use to talk to the strugglers among us:

1. **He uses a story to convict David.** *Stories are powerful. They make the point without being confrontational. It may be a story that serves to illustrate the point. It may be a story of someone in a similar situation. It may be a story from your life.*
2. **Nathan speaks the word of the Lord.** *Always use Scripture. Let God's Word convict and accuse, not you. This helps keep it from becoming personal.*
3. **He reminded David of all the Lord had done for him.** *Salvation, blessings, and previous deliverance.*
4. **Nathan makes clear that David's sin showed he despised the word of God and thus even God Himself.** *Sin is always about your relationship with God.*

5. **Then Nathan spells out consequences.** *Sometimes I do this to illustrate what happens if confession and repentance do not occur. After all, salvation may be at stake. Or the marriage. Or a job. It's also a time to be honest about inevitable consequences, legal consequences, church consequences, and financial consequences.*

Not everyone reacts like David. Some of those in the composite story last chapter did not. I have looked people in the eye and spoken truth into their life when I was not sure what the reaction would be. I have been yelled at, threatened, cussed out, and had my own sins thrown in my face. I have heard an endless stream of excuses in attempts to justify what has happened. People have even pleaded with me to help cover up their sin.

However, most people react like David. Some almost immediately. Others take some time to come to grips with who they really want to be and what they have done. Even some of the ones who react badly later own up to their sin and ask for help.

I have been where David was. I have been where Nathan was.

So, as those involved in redeeming sinful believers, we must do two things:

1. *Continue to stress the truth of forgiveness because that is the only thing that will overcome the guilt and shame.*
2. *Help them manage the consequences, because there will be consequences.* ■

Repent Is an Action Verb

John Bernardone was a rich playboy living in central Italy around 1300 A.D. The only way for life to be much better would be if he had also been a war hero. So when John's village went to war, he expected to return a hero. Except he got sick and spent the battle in a hospital tent. He did a lot of thinking about God, Jesus, and how he wanted to live his life. And he decided to change his life—to repent.

He decided to live his life based on three great principles: poverty, purity, and preaching. I do need to say that these are great alliterative points for a sermon in English. I am not sure how they sounded in Italian, but . . .

Poverty. His father was a wealthy cloth merchant, so John took the inventory available, sold it all, and gave the proceeds to the poor.

Purity. He was so committed to this that he and followers traveled in groups, not as individuals. That way no one would be tempted without others there to help.

Preaching. He loved talking about God so much that if there were no people around, he would preach his sermon to the nearby birds.

And he made one of the all-time great statements about evangelism.

"Speak about Jesus always. Use words when necessary."

You may be wondering why you have never heard of John Bernardone. Because when people talk about him, they use the name he was better known by in church history: Francis of Assisi.

Repentance is not just an emotion. It is not just a change of attitude. It is more than being sorry.

Real repentance is being sorry enough to quit and start again with the life you want to live. Sorry enough to change. Sorry enough to live life in a different way.

Francis of Assisi got it.

A Word to the Helpers

This is where the process gets difficult. Repentance is where the strugglers start putting their confession into action. It will require you to be wise, patient, understanding, forgiving, and to hold them accountable.

This is where the hard work begins. ■

CHAPTER FIVE

Change Is Hard

I've never appreciated somebody blowing smoke when trying to talk to me about my struggles. I want real talk from real people. I want people who know what they're talking about: people who have the scars to prove it and have battled their own demons or spent lots of time helping others battle theirs.

I am now one of those people. I will tell you that most churches have those people. Those whose wounds are now scars. People who *want* to help. Who *will* help.

Charles Got It

I have known Charles my whole life. I've always had a lot of respect and admiration for him, but you always do for the genuinely good guys.

Charles did not plan to go into full-time ministry. It was a second career for him. He has done a lot of quality ministry over the years, much of which I got to see up close and personal at various times. He has always been organized, committed, a hard worker, and driven to see kingdom success. He loves his Lord, his family, and church people.

He called me one day to tell me what was going on in his life. He had fallen into a pattern of addictive sin, and he was in the process of reaching out to different people he thought could help.

Charles had confessed his sin. His family knew. His elders knew. They were all standing by him. He was continuing to work on staff at his church.

He was also actively working on repentance: not just being sorry, not just confessing his struggle. He was committed to life change, so he could be the follower of Jesus he desired to be. He even went on a week-long retreat to focus on intensive spiritual counseling to help jump start his recovery.

He called me because he was getting all the help he could, but he needed to talk to someone who had... well, messed up their life. He knew me, loved me, and knew I loved him. He knew much of my story and had been consistent in his support and encouragement to me. He knew I had made it. He knew that God had redeemed and restored me.

I was important to his repentance journey, but not because he had to have my help, but because he knew that I got it. I knew him. He knew that I cared about the real him and that I would not confuse his identity with what he had done.

I was the living witness to grace and mercy, not judgment, shame, and condemnation, because those were what God had given me through Jesus. Maybe he just needed to see scars, so he could know what his wounds would someday become.

I wasn't shocked by what happened to Charles because we all sin, and none of us is immune to the possibility that sin could take over parts of our life, try to pull us out of the light.

However, I also was not at all surprised about his repentance; his active work to fix things spiritually, because Charles is a believer and that is what believers do. We love God enough to fix it when we get off track.

I love and respect Charles even more because I watched him fight for his faith. He's still doing effective ministry in his community of faith, and he's still helping people be better disciples. Even though he's past the age when most men retire, he's still in the ministry trenches, because he knows what God has done for him.

But Repenting Is Such Hard Work

Correct, and so far, all the stories I have shared have been about people who whipped their demons or at least never quit fighting them. The only exception is "Fred." He never would confess or repent, but I want to be honest about the hard work that goes into repentance. Repentance is an action, not just a feeling. Sometimes you can even see it register in their face as it dawns on them how difficult and how much work is involved in really repenting.

There is a "last resort" verse that I have found helpful to get people to wake up and get about the business of repenting. It's also a verse that is full of encouragement to those who just cannot get past their struggles, but still keep fighting for their faith.

It is a passage with a dire warning and a passage of great encouragement. The warning is this:

> 4 For it is impossible, in the case of those who have once been enlightened, who have tasted the heavenly gift, and have shared in the Holy Spirit, 5 and have tasted the goodness of the word of God and the powers of the age to come, 6 and then have fallen away, to restore them again to repentance, since they are crucifying once again the Son of God to their own harm and holding him up to contempt. 7 For land that has drunk the rain that often falls on it, and produces a crop useful to those for whose sake it is cultivated, receives a blessing from God. 8 But if it bears thorns and thistles, it is worthless and near to being cursed, and its end is to be burned (Hebrews 6:4-8).

This is addressed to believers, so I start by reminding you of the blessings you have in Jesus: blessings you will forfeit if you do not repent. We have been enlightened in a dark world, and we want to walk in the light where our sins are forgiven. We've tasted the heavenly gift. Jesus—God's gift. It's a little heaven on earth if you will. We've shared in the Holy Spirit. We've tasted the goodness of the Word of God. We've glimpsed the powers of the age to come.

This is a good time to list the blessings God has given you. In dark times, it may be hard to see them, but you know the blessings in your life. You must realize what is at stake—and what you will lose unless you repent.

It's impossible to restore to repentance the ones who've fallen away. What is the point of trying to restore someone if it is impossible? I most often hear this from those who haven't been in church for years and from those whose sin has been repetitive. Is there hope? Or is it impossible to repent?

Please hear this: If you are talking/confessing/wrestling with repentance, you haven't fallen away. Something (the Holy Spirit perhaps) within you continues to wrestle with following Jesus. Even as you are trying to decide what to do, God is giving you yet another opportunity. Do not waste it.

I don't know exactly where that line of "too fallen to come back" is. After all, I am not God. I do know Him, however, and if you refuse to confess and repent, there will come a point where you can't—won't—come back. It isn't possible.

Repentance is difficult work. It is hard, but there are severe consequences to failing to repent. You lose the blessings listed. You can get to a point from which you cannot come back.

Jesus died on the cross for your sins. Christians who refuse to repent, who in effect flaunt their sin, disgrace Jesus. It's neither your disgrace nor disgrace to the church that the Hebrew writer is talking about. You're disgracing Jesus. You're shaming Him by your refusal to repent.

But You Have a Choice

It doesn't have to be that way. You have a choice. Here is the next part of that passage:

> [7] For land that has drunk the rain that often falls on it, and produces a crop useful to those for whose sake it is cultivated, receives a blessing from God. [8] But if it bears thorns and thistles, it is worthless and near to being cursed, and its end is to be burned (Hebrews 6:7-8).

This may remind you of the story Jesus told on the kinds of soil the good news falls upon. In Matthew 13, Jesus talks about soil. The Hebrews writer does here, too. Good land receives the rain and produces a useful crop for those farming it. God blesses it. Or... the land produces thorns and thistles and is worthless. It is near to being cursed (impossible to repent) and in the end is burned.

Blessed and blessing others. Restored to usefulness.

Cursed and burned.

And you get to decide. Choose the kind of soil you are going to be.

Here Is The Good News

I think you will make the right choice. I believe in you. Just like the Hebrew writer was confident in the struggling Christians to whom he was writing. This is a passage I would read over and over looking for confidence that things could be different in my life. That things would be different:

> [9] Though we speak in this way, yet in your case, beloved, we feel sure of better things—things that belong to salvation. [10] For God is not unjust so as to overlook your work and the love that you have shown for his name in serving the saints, as you still do (Hebrews 6:9-10).

In spite of the warning, I remain confident of better things from you. Those better things are the things of salvation. You are going to make the right choice and be saved. God is not unjust. He will not overlook your work and the love you have shown for His name by serving Christians. Even as you still do.

That is the whole point of this book. Faithful Christians can get off track—way off track. It's hard to admit (confess) that. It is hard to do something about it (repent). But you have done things for the Lord. You have cared for people. God won't forget that.

So Put Your Repentance into Action

> [11] And we desire each one of you to show the same earnestness to have the full assurance of hope until the end, [12] so that you may not be sluggish, but imitators of those who through faith and patience inherit the promises (Hebrews 6:11-12).

Start to work. Be earnest and diligent. Be alert to Satan, the hungry lion. Pay attention. Correct the ways you are not in the light. Confess and repent. Then stay after it until the end when our hope in Christ will be realized. Do not quit. Do not get lazy.

Imitate those whose faith and patience lead them to inherit what we have been promised. The people who are encouraging you. The people in your faith community who will help you.

Listen to my story and the stories of others. Be like me. Be like Charles. We aren't perfect, but we are confident in our hope. Do not quit. Make the right choice every day. Right up until the end.

Even If It Requires Radical Surgery

It is a hard decision to commit that you will do whatever it takes to defeat the demons in your life. It is even harder to follow through on that commitment. Because sometimes it takes radical surgery to save the patient. Remember the story of my melanoma from the introduction. Radical surgery.

Jesus said it this way:

> [29] If your right eye causes you to sin, tear it out and throw it away. For it is better lose one of your members than that your whole body be thrown into hell. [30] And if your right hand causes you to sin, cut it off and throw it away. For it is better that you lose one of your members than that your whole body go into hell (Matthew 5:29-30).

When I committed to do whatever it took to be the man God wants me to be, I had to evaluate a number of things. One of those was my career as a preacher. Many of my struggles took place in the context of local, full-time ministry. It was hard to think about. Preaching was the only thing I really ever wanted to do. It was the only career I was trained to do, and it was the only thing I was any good at doing.

I had to wonder if that context had anything to do with the struggle. I had to evaluate if I could even address my sin in that environment. Was my job part of the problem? I realized that being faithful to Jesus was far more important than being a preacher. Being faithful as a husband and father was way more important than any job.

So, I quit full-time ministry. It was hard. There was always a church somewhere wanting to hire me. Most of them knew why I quit, but wanted me anyway. I still had a family to support, but had no idea what to do for a living. I fumbled around for a while trying to figure it out. I moved from sales, yard work, roofing, phone book delivery to finally settling in Yellow Page advertising sales for about 10 years.

God took care of us the whole time. There was always enough money. Interestingly, I still did a lot of preaching and ministry, mostly for free. I did fill-in preaching, interim preaching, and for several years, I preached on Wednesday nights to a group of 500-600 university students—for no pay. Our church asked me to serve as an elder, which I did for many years. Eventually, I went back into full-time ministry. It wasn't local work; it was as a traveling evangelist. Could I have gone back into full-time local work without any problems? Maybe. Probably. But I never wanted to take that chance. It's better to be safe than sorry. And the wounds had become scars.

But What About You?

So what might your radical surgery look like? Here are a few of the "surgeries" I have seen over the years:

- *Changing careers*
- *Changing jobs*
- *Cutting out cable*
- *No playing—or coaching—sports*
- *No online shopping*
- *No overnight trips for work*
- *No alcohol*

I do not know what things might cause you to stumble. I do not know the environment that is dangerous for you. But you do. You have to figure it out. You have to be honest, and ruthless. Let nothing come between you and Jesus. It's better to lose a career than your soul.

Real repentance may require radical surgery, but it's so worth it. And you can do it.

Because Jesus Will Help You

Confession and repentance are hard to do because we project the way we feel onto others. We assume everyone sees us a certain way because that is how we see ourselves. We even do this with God. When you really come to terms with your sin, and you commit to do whatever it takes to repent, it is still hard to accept the truth about God and Jesus. I never doubted how much God loved me. I never doubted that He knew me even better than I knew myself. (He still does.) I even clung to the truth that God knew my heart, knew how much I really love Him, and how much I want to walk in the light. However, when it came time to consciously confess my sin to God, it was hard to get past the guilt and shame. It was hard to admit that I could not fix myself even though I wanted to. In a strange way, it was hard to ask God for help.

Maybe you have had those confused feelings when trying to talk to the Holy God you promised to serve.

Listen to this:

> [14] Since then we have a great high priest who has passed through the heavens, Jesus, the Son of God, let us hold fast our confession. [15] For we do not have a high priest who is unable to sympathize with our weaknesses, but one who in every respect has been tempted as we are, yet without sin. [16] Let us then with confidence draw near to the throne of grace, that we may receive mercy and find grace to help in time of need (Hebrews 4:14-16).

Jesus is our High Priest, the One who represents us before God. Jesus goes into the presence of God on our behalf. Hold on tightly to your confession of faith. Do not let go.

Jesus gets it. He was here and lived among us. He was tempted in every way just like us. Remember those three areas of the world we cannot love: appetites, greed, pride. He faced all of them, but He never sinned. That's the difference. He can sympathize with our weakness because He has been here. He will not endorse our sin, not gloss over our failures, not accept it as the way we are. But He does understand our struggle. He understands your struggle.

Maybe that is why this passage is in our Bible—so we will know that Jesus gets it. He understands. Go before God's throne with confidence. When you really want to be different and are ready to change, go. Be confident that you'll find grace to help. You'll be granted forgiveness in spite of yourself. It isn't just a one-time transaction for your latest sin, but grace that transforms and empowers you for change.

Jesus understands your struggle. Grace is extended for your forgiveness. Mercy is given to open wide the opportunity to change. Real repentance.

A Word to the Helpers

Richard really was one of the greatest elders I ever knew. He had a shepherd's heart, but he could never understand people who made a mess of their marriage. He had a great marriage and wanted everyone else to have what he and his wife had. The problem was that he would say that publicly. He would talk about how great his marriage was and that did encourage married couples to aspire to that kind of marriage. Then he would talk about his greatest shock as an elder was how many marriages were in trouble. He would then explain how he just couldn't understand it.

He really did hurt over struggling marriages. He cried over failed marriages and wanted them to be better. He'd do anything to help them, but he never could figure out why none of his flock came to him with their marriage problems. He really did care; he just did not get why they did not seek him out. But who wants to go to someone for help when you are sure they will not understand?

We have to do a better job of letting the strugglers know we are there for them, that we understand, and we will help.

I was once part of a church like that. I served as one of the leaders there for several years. We had a reputation among the Christians in our city. We were often referred to as the church where "the screwed-up people go." I know that most of the time that was said in a disparaging way, but the truth was, I liked that reputation.

I would often repeat it, adding that it was true but we didn't want everyone to stay like that, and that we would help them change. I would often make this statement publicly in our worship assemblies.

"If you are in a mess, please come talk to one of your elders or our wives. We will love you; we will speak truth into your life; we will walk with you. You have not done anything that one of us—or someone we love deeply—has not done. We are living proof that God forgives. And if you think you have done something so bad you are ashamed to talk to one of us, then come see me. You cannot have messed up your life any more than I have my life, and God has healed me. He can do that for you."

The strugglers among us have to know that forgiveness and healing are possible. That lives can change. That God does put broken lives together again.

Because we are living proof. We, too, were once wounded by our sin.

But Jesus has turned those wounds into scars. ■

CHAPTER SIX

Confession in Action

That's a great definition of repentance: confession in action. It should be clear by now that repentance is so much more than "I am sorry I did it." Repentance is where the confession gets real. It is where you must live out your intention to be a different person. It's difficult, and it's messy.

This Couple Gets It

I knew them, but not well. They were one of those sweet, never-miss-church, older couples that sat near us in worship. I often said hello to them, but never had any in-depth conversations. One Sunday during our prayer time, they called me over to meet their grandchildren. The grands were all in their mid- to late teens, and their grandmother was so happy they had come to church with them.

She introduced me and asked if I would pray over them. That in itself is a little awkward. Teenagers and this old church guy they don't know. It became a little more awkward when she asked if I would specifically pray for them to find Jesus. Though uncomfortable, she was so intentional and sweet that I prayed that prayer.

It is really special that over the next couple of years at least three people (that I know of) were baptized into Christ as a result of the process that began that day. One of them even worked for the church as our nursery coordinator for a time.

The Story Gets Even Better

This is a neat story that gets even better. I was talking about this couple with our preacher once, and he asked if I knew their backstory. Here is what he told me, and it is an amazing story of repentance.

This was the second marriage for each of them. They were Christians who had evidently not been active in their faith. After they got married, there came a time when they desired to come back into the light. I have no idea of all the work that must have gone into what happened next, but here it is. They had both given end-of-life care to their previous spouses. That is real repentance in action—doing what they felt God called them to do. Living out their love.

They did not just talk about coming back to the Lord, they lived out a faithful life in extraordinary ways.

Repentance Is Life Changing

Repentance is the work of changing your life to be more of an "in the light" believer. We have written quite a bit about the fact that all these decisions are heart decisions. Sin is ultimately a heart issue; so are confession and repentance. You are working on your heart and making decisions that reflect true love. Let me suggest another area to work on in your repentance.

Work on changing your mind in a positive way:

> [1] I appeal to you therefore, brothers, by the mercies of God, to present your bodies as a living sacrifice, holy and acceptable to God, which is your spiritual worship. [2] Do not be conformed to this world, but be transformed by the renewal of your mind, that by testing you may discern what is the will of God, what is good and acceptable and perfect (Romans 12:1-2).

Continue to keep God's mercy in view. Live in the light. Love God from the heart. It is much easier to live the way you desire if you keep focused on what God has done for you. Be thankful every day that your sins are forgiven.

Offer your body to God as a living sacrifice made holy by Jesus. Heart, mind, and body. This is how you live out your repentance.

When I was in college, my roommate, Richard, put a sign above our door that would be visible every time we walked out of our room. It was this verse:

> [20] I have been crucified with Christ. It is no longer I who live, but Christ who lives in me. And the life I now live in the flesh I live by faith in the Son of God, who loved me and gave himself for me (Galatians 2:20).

It is a mindset that you cultivate every day. That mindset is then reflected in how you live. The same Paul who wrote this passage writes something similar in Romans 6. There he talks about dying with Christ (being crucified) in baptism. He then explains how that plays out in life:

> [12] Let not sin therefore reign in your mortal body, to make you obey its passions (Romans 6:12).

This is what David and Bathsheba failed to do. Instead, they let sin and passion rule their bodies, not God. As the Galatians passage reminds us, it is not us, but Christ living in us. We live by faith in Jesus, not in ourselves. It's paradoxical to say, but it is easier to live when I have already died. Crucified with Christ yet alive in Him.

This is different from how the world lives, which brings us back to the Romans 12 passage. Do not be conformed to the world. Do not be driven by your appetites, by the things you want, by your ego and pride. Instead, transform yourself by renewing you mind. Fill your mind with the right things. The good and holy things. Read your Bible. Pray. Listen to—and sing—praise music. Have Jesus conversations.

When you focus on living your love, and you fill your mind with things that reflect that love, it is much easier to bring your body in line with that. Heart. Mind. Body.

Repentance is confession in action.

Another Story from My Friend, Peter

It may be my favorite story in the Bible. Well, one of them anyway. It is a faith story that starts with what seems to be a tragedy that ends up a great story, which is what much of my life looks like at times. Maybe yours does. too. Let's learn a lesson or two from my friend, Peter. Found in Matthew 14, it reveals a blueprint for sin, confession, repentance, and restoration.

Jesus had sent the disciples to cross the lake without Him. He stayed to spend some time alone in prayer (a great lesson in and of itself). It was a tough journey. The wind was up; the waves were rough. Late in the night/very early morning, Jesus went to them, not in a boat, but walking on the water. Let that sink in a minute. Never forget how awesome, amazing, and powerful is the One you follow. The disciples got scared and thought maybe a ghost was out on the water, which is a little odd since they had just seen Jesus feed 5,000 people with five loaves and two fish. After all, you would think they would know Who had the kind of power that would let you walk on water.

You already get the lesson here. Jesus is always with us. We just don't always recognize Him. That's especially true when the going gets tough and things are scary—like when you have failed to live as you intended. He does not desert you. He is not afraid of your rough seas. And He walks on the water! Maybe they were scared because they were not looking for—or at—Jesus. Or maybe they just didn't expect Him in the storm. But He was there.

"Have courage. It is me. Don't be afraid."

That is what He says to you in the storm. I am with you. Be brave. Stop being afraid.

Then Peter made an astounding statement of faith.

"If it is you, tell me to come to you."

And Jesus told him to come.

Why ask? I don't think Peter was looking for accolades or to just experience the thrill of walking on water. I don't think he spent much time thinking it through. I think he saw Jesus and wanted to be with Him and do great things with Him. So he asked. You've had those moments of great faith, including when you decided to be baptized and follow Jesus. There have been other moments of commitment and resolve, and many times you acted on those decisions.

Never forget your great adventures of faith when you stepped out of the boat and onto the water as Peter did. What a great story! You've had those moments when you and God did amazing things in and for the kingdom. I have too. Just like Peter did when he walked on the water.

Until He Didn't

Oops.

Peter saw how windy it was and got scared and started to sink. Of course he got scared. If you are going to walk on the water, at least do it on a calm day without wind or waves. Peter, though, walked in the middle of a storm. Fear and doubt must have crept into his mind until it overwhelmed him, and he just stopped. Then he began sinking. It all started because he took his eyes off Jesus and started looking at the storm instead. Remember David! His problems came when he wasn't focused on what he was supposed to be doing. Just like all of us. When we let our eyes drift from Jesus, trouble follows. Maybe your heart is not as attuned to Jesus as it should be. Satan is out there prowling around like a roaring lion. Fear and doubt enter, and that is where Satan's lies gain traction.

"I'll never find someone to share my life with... "

"How can I ever pay my bills... ?"

"What does everyone think of me... "

You get the picture. Fear, doubts, and Satan. And before you realize it, you are drowning.

Thankfully, Peter's story did not end there. He knew what to do. He cried out for the Lord to save him. Confession. If you want your wounds to heal, there is only one answer... Jesus. Not you. Not more work. Not the church. Not people. Not even a book. Not even a book written by a great sinner who found grace. Only Jesus. Confession and repentance. All the things we share in this book about defeating your demons and being healed are based on one thing—Jesus.

It was Jesus who reached out His hand for Peter. Growing up with this story, I think I had the impression that Peter walked to Jesus, started visiting, and noticed the wind. Then he sank, and Jesus reached down and hauled him up. I am not sure it happened that way anymore. If Peter was standing right by Jesus, he would have grabbed Him on the way down and hung on for dear life, which would still be a pretty good story. Grab Jesus and hang on.

I suspect, however, that Peter was still on his way to Jesus when he started sinking. Jesus likely ran to him so when Peter called out, Jesus was right there. He is right there with you, too. Just waiting for you to call out in confession and reach out in repentance. He will hear and answer your cry. Maybe God will send someone into your life to help you find your way back to Jesus. But it will be Jesus who is there to save you from drowning. Take His hand and do not let go. Ever!

Then Jesus cut right to the heart of the matter by telling Peter he did not show much faith. Jesus asked him why he doubted. So... what has happened to your faith? Are you doubting your Jesus decision? That is the real question here. Do you still want Jesus? Still believe in Him? Repentance is turning back to the light. And then walking toward—and into—that light with all your heart.

The story ends with Jesus and Peter climbing back into the boat. Do you know how they got back to the boat? They walked. Peter walked on the water again. This time Jesus was right beside him, and he didn't sink.

Please know this. Jesus is not through with you. He still longs to do amazing kingdom things with you and through you.

That starts by focusing on Jesus and hanging on while you walk on the water.

A Word of Encouragement

It can be a little discouraging if we are going to be honest. Repentance is hard work, and it takes time. It is easy to let doubt and fear creep in—easy to start believing the lies from Satan. Allow me to share what I believe to be one of the greatest encouragement passages in the entire Bible:

> 1 Therefore, since we are surrounded by so great a cloud of witnesses, let us also lay aside every weight, and sin which clings so closely, and let us run with endurance the race that is set before us, 2 looking to Jesus, the founder and perfecter of our faith, who for the joy that was set before him endured the cross, despising the shame, and is seated at the right hand of the throne of God (Hebrews 12:1-2).

I do not even know who wrote the book of Hebrews, but I am so glad the Holy Spirit used him to write this passage. It has meant so much to me on my journey. Without fail, it has proved to be a blessing to those I have worked with in the battle to turn wounds into scars.

We are surrounded by a great crowd of witnesses. You have people surrounding you who are rooting for you. People who have made it to the finish line. This encouragement comes right after Hebrews 11—the great heroes of faith chapter. They are watching you fight for your faith. They are cheering you on. Noah, Abraham, Enoch, and Abel. All of them wre great people of faith; some of them were great sinners; but they were all people of great faith. David is in that crowd. So are people like my Dad, my in-laws, and my friend, Foy. Great people of faith and great sinners. Faith fighters who made it. It is like a track stadium with the stands full of people cheering you on until you finish the race and join them.

Throw off everything that hinders your race. Like David did, throw off the sin that so easily entangles you. Run with perseverance the race laid out for you. It is hard, but here is the secret: Do not quit. Don't give up. Put one foot in front of the other until you finish. All of those heroes of faith who have gone before are cheering you on. Those of us still in the race with you are cheering you on, too.

Fix your eyes on Jesus. Boy, that sounds like Peter, who by the way is cheering you on, too. Keep your heart focused. Run in the light. Jesus is the author and perfecter of our faith. We are complete in Him. He knew the joy that was before Him, and so do you. Because Jesus kept the end goal in sight, He was able to endure the pain of the cross. He scorned that shame. He made it to the throne of God. Keep your eyes on that goal.

Think about how Jesus endured the opposition of sinful men. You may have to endure some things from people who are not helping you. Do not listen to those who tell you that you cannot be forgiven, that you cannot get into heaven. Endure it when someone tries to define you by your sin or your past. They are wrong, and they are opposing Jesus.

Do not grow weary. You are running a spiritual marathon, not a sprint.

Turn your heart to God. Keep your eyes on Jesus.

Listen to the cheers as you run your race.

See who is waiting at the finish line.

Do not quit. Because you are forgiven.

You have confessed, and you are living your repentance.

A Word to the Helpers

I think it is wise for us to remember that people in crisis are in the middle of their storm much like the storm the disciples were navigating when Jesus went to them. They are ashamed, scared, confused, and maybe they do not even recognize Jesus at that moment. We are there to point them to Jesus. So let's remember how Jesus spoke to His disciples.

Jesus did not condemn them, yell at them, or lecture them. They were scared, and even though He must have been frustrated and disappointed, He simply reassured them.

Do likewise. ■

Forgiveness Is Not an Option

If you have read this far, it should be abundantly clear that God has forgiven you. There are three things in your life that absolutely remove all doubt. You are walking in the light. Or returned to walk in the light. You have confessed your sin to your God. And you have repented. You are willing—and you are doing—the hard work involved in changing your life. God has forgiven you. He said it, and you must believe it.

Over the next two chapters, we will explore various aspects of what it means to be forgiven. To live forgiven. To live in a community with the forgiven. You will be reminded of the reality that God forgives and what that means in your life. Real forgiveness comes from God. He alone has the power to ensure your sins are never held against you. That is why we pray the model prayer from the Sermon on the Mount. Asking God to forgive our sins, debts, and trespasses. Asking not to be led into temptation. Asking to be delivered from the evil one. It is a prayer of commitment to walk in the light and stay in the light. It is a confession that we know where the source of healing is.

But we ask to be forgiven as we forgive those who sin against us. We need to explore that also. How do we relate to the sinners among us? You forgive others, God forgives you. You do not forgive others, God does not forgive you. Let me be clear about this. We are not God. I am not God and you are not God. My forgiving someone has nothing to do with their relationship with God. That is God's business. But it does have everything to do with my relationship with God:

> [12] and forgive us our debts, as we also have forgiven our debtors. [13] And lead us not into temptation, but deliver us from evil. [14] For if you forgive others their trespasses, your heavenly Father will also forgive you, [15] but if you do not forgive others their trespasses, neither will your Father forgive your trespasses (Matthew 6:12-15).

It doesn't get any plainer than this. But here is a word to the struggler about extending forgiveness. You will have people sin against you. Gossip. Anger. Unloving and unforgiving Christians. You must forgive them. It is acceptable to have a conversation about what they are doing to you, but you must forgive. It is not about whether they ask, or even deserve, forgiveness. It is not about playing God. His forgiveness is a whole different matter. You can only control your confession and repentance.

Forgive if you want to be forgiven.

A Word to the Helpers

How do you feel about the struggling sinner among you? Do you want them to heal? Will you acknowledge God's forgiveness in their lives? Will you forgive? Can you get past the judgmental attitude? Will you hold their sin/s over them? Is your forgiveness conditional? Are sinners welcome in your church? Are sinners welcome in your life?

Of course, I am talking about confessional, penitent sinners. Yes, consequences will still have to be managed and handled. You can *express* frustration, hurt, disappointment. However, you must *experience* love, forgiveness, and acceptance. ■

Live Forgiven

Satan wants to be God. He is not, and he knows it. So... he wants to use you to embarrass God to make a mockery of what Jesus did on the cross. He wants to separate you from God and keep you away from Him. But he uses the same tricks over and over and over again. He lies.

We sin. We repent. We confess. God forgives.

So if Satan cannot keep us locked in our sin, he wants to lie to us about our forgiveness.

Everything we are talking about in this book can be found in one story. It is a tragic story full of hope. Of course, it should cover everything because it is the story where it all started. You can read it for yourself at the start of the Bible in Genesis 2 and 3.

Where It All Began

God created a perfect world. We messed it up. God promised to fix it, and He did. That basically sums up the story, and we are still living in the reality of that story. Adam and Eve live in the Garden of this perfect world. They work in the Garden, and they live in relationship with God. In the middle of the Garden is the tree of Life. It's pretty important because, well... life. There's also the tree of the Knowledge of Good and Evil. Adam and Eve can eat from any tree in the Garden except the Knowledge tree. God told them if they ate of that tree, they would die. Satan comes as a serpent to ruin God's creation. He uses the same blueprint and pattern with Adam and Eve that he uses today with you. Yes, he is still trying to destroy God's creation. The roaring lion still wants to separate you from God and get you out of the light.

Here are a few lessons from this story that might apply to your situation. I sure learned a lot from it.

The Temptation

Satan wants you to doubt God.

"Did God really say. . . ?" That is still a struggle today. We Christians live in a culture that mocks God in an attempt to justify behavior that goes against God's will. It is a common thing for us to convince ourselves that God is not really opposed to our behavior.

"You will not die." Satan lied. He is the father of lies, so of course he lied. It is easy to convince ourselves there will not be consequences to our actions. Listening to the lies of Satan.

Satan uses the things of the world to entice Adam and Eve to sin. You do remember the three things of the world with which we cannot fall in love.

The fruit of the tree is good for food. Physical appetites. Hunger. Of course, they have a whole garden of choices, but Satan wants their attention focused on the "forbidden fruit."

It is pleasing to the eye. Greed. The desire to have what appeals to us. Wanting what is not ours.

Satan tells them yet another lie. You'll gain wisdom and be like God. Pride and ego. You can be god. In control of your life and destiny.

The Sin

Eve gave in first. She took the fruit and ate it. Then she gave it to

Adam, and he ate. And it was true—they obtained knowledge. They now knew about good and evil, which means they had to make choices. They now knew they were naked, so they sewed some coverings.

Wait. If Adam was there, why did he not stop Eve? Why didn't he say anything? Did she have the audacity to do what Adam was afraid to do? Was he waiting to see what happened? We do have a responsibility to each other to warn of danger. Eve failed, but Adam failed twice. He did not warn Eve, and then he also sinned.

Eve needed Adam to watch out for her, and he needed her. Ultimately, she gave in, then invited him. Sin often ends up involving other people, either directly or indirectly. Then Adam and Eve heard God calling them. So they did the logical thing, which was not logical at all. They hid. Why do we think we can hide from God? I often wonder if that is why some strugglers stop attending worship. Do they think they can avoid God if they don't go to His house?

God was asking where they were. Interesting. He knew where they were. He was asking, so they would face the consequences of their decision. They quickly moved from a relationship with their Creator to hiding because they were naked. Aware now not just of physical realities, but spiritual nakedness. From in the light to out of the light. God points out that He knew by asking who told them they were naked. Then He asks if they had eaten of the tree, opening the door for confession.

The Blame Game

Adam blames Eve. It was the woman. How many times have you attempted to avoid facing your sin by blaming someone else? *They seduced me. The money was just left out in the open. Everyone else was doing it.* Of course, Satan uses other people to tempt us. He used Eve to entice Adam into sin. But ultimately our sin is because of our choice. God always provides an exit ramp to get off the sin road. He did for David. He did for me. He has for you. As we have talked about, at some point you must own your sin.

Adam even blamed God, at least indirectly. He blamed Eve, but he did point out that it was God who gave Eve to him. So... if you want to be technical, it was God's fault. You know how that goes. Telling God that He made you that way. Whatever the sin is you can find a way to blame God for creating you with certain appetites. Or for making certain things in this world so desirable. And on and on it goes. How often do we blame God because we turned something good into something evil.

What about Eve? She blamed the devil. *The serpent made me. The temptation was just too great. No one could have resisted.* Those are the same excuses we use today to avoid confession.

God's Answer Was to Fix Their Mess

God explains how He will fix things. Eve will have a descendent Who will destroy the devil by crushing his head. Her descendent will have His heel bruised, so there will be some pain and suffering, but Satan will die. There it is. The announcement of the cross. God's own Son will be born of a woman (Eve's descendant), and though it will require His death (bruising His heel), He will destroy Satan. Forgiveness of sins, resurrection, and eternal life. Crushing the head of the devil. It was all right there from the beginning.

Consequences

Sin does have consequences. Adam and Eve have to leave the Garden, including the tree of life. Death is now present. Adam has to work hard to feed his family. Eve will have pain in childbirth. All of these consequences are still in effect today. They are true.

It's also true that Jesus came and lived among us. He did die for our sins. God did raise Him from the dead. Satan is defeated. We are forgiven.

This story still plays out over and over again. It did in my life. It has in your life. Great sinners and great grace.

Like this.

But I Am the Worst Sinner Ever

We all sin. Obviously, you are incredibly aware of your own sin, and you're aware of others' sins. Some people use that awareness as an excuse. *Well, at least I am not as bad as so-and-so.* Sometimes, though, we look at ourselves and think that no one has ever done anything as bad as we have. Maybe because we see up close the consequences of our sin. Maybe we just feel the guilt and remorse so deeply. Maybe even our repentance and confession make us feel pain over what we should have been or done. It becomes a battle for healthy spiritual self-image. I still struggle sometimes with the, "I am the worst sinner ever" syndrome. I am not the only one.

Listen to what Paul the Apostle wrote,

> [15] The saying is trustworthy and deserving of full acceptance, that Christ Jesus came into the world to save sinners, of whom I am the foremost. [16] But I received mercy for this reason, that in me, as the foremost, Jesus Christ might display his perfect patience as an example to those who were to believe in him for eternal life (1 Timothy 1:15-16).

Let's start with the one basic truth to which we can cling: Jesus came to save sinners. That is why Jesus came. He did lots of things while on this earth, but His reason for coming was to save us sinners. Of course non-believers need to hear this truth, but that message is not just for the non-Christian. His blood keeps cleansing (saving) us as we walk in the light and seek to follow Him. It is still a true statement that you are saved from your sins.

Paul identifies himself as the foremost, the chief, of sinners. Oops. He must have meant that he used to be the worst of sinners. You know, the whole persecuting Christians thing. But he does not say "was," he says "am." I do not believe Paul made a mistake. I do not think the Holy Spirit missed one here. Paul said what he meant and what he often felt. Maybe he still wrestled with the whole "what I hate is what I do" struggle. Maybe he is haunted by his past.

Here is the takeaway for those of you struggling to live up to your calling in Christ. This is a reminder of something that is true and that you should make a part of your life. Jesus came to save sinners. You are a sinner. You are saved.

Maybe it is OK to remember what you were: the greatest of sinners. Just don't live there. Use that as a reminder of God's grace. Use that as motivation to praise the Lord for His goodness and mercy. And stay alert. We are all sinners that Jesus is saving. It is why recovering alcoholics refer to themselves as sober alcoholics, even if they haven't had a drink in 20 years.

I also get what Paul meant when he said God shows mercy to him, the foremost of sinners. Jesus is showing His unlimited patience in him as an example. Me too. As you have read these stories, and there are more to come, you realize that there is something powerful about the testimony of a healed, forgiven sinner.

If you are in the battle right now, know that you will come out victorious and forgiven. God still has something for you to do. Just like He did with David, Peter, Charles, me... and you. You may always wish things had not happened the way they did, but you will have an amazing testimony to God's grace and forgiveness

Just be sure to stay in the light.

Caught in the Act

I have no idea what it was that started you on the road to confession. For many of us, it was a realization that we could not continue the way we were going. We were not living as the people we wanted to be or who we really were. For others, it was an intervention by someone that loved you and believed in you. Someone wanted you to live in the light. And of course, some of you were caught. You may have been confronted by someone who found evidence of your struggle. Maybe it was an unexpected audit, a DUI, an overheard comment or conversation, or a text message. Something pointed to your sin. Other times, you get caught in the act.

It is a strange story all the way around. You can read it in John 8. Well, you can sort of read it. You will notice that the passage comes with an asterisk. That's a note that this story is not found in the earliest manuscripts. It may not have been in the original text. So how did it get in the Bible? I assume someone inserted it. I do not know why. Then it got copied and copied until it just seemed to belong. Why did no one say take it out? Maybe it was because everyone knew the story. It may have really happened. After all, Jesus did many more amazing things than are written in the Bible. John himself said if you wrote down everything that Jesus did, the whole world could not contain the books. So, I think we have an authentic story from the life of Jesus, and it teaches us so much about sin and forgiveness.

What Happened?

I don't know her name, but she was caught in the act of adultery. *Caught in the act.* It wasn't that a person saw someone's donkey parked outside her house, saw her going in the wrong house, or had some indication that something was going on. *Caught in the act.* Even more humiliating, the religious leaders and teachers of the law were the ones who caught her. They hauled her into the temple courts where Jesus was teaching the people. Not only did she get caught in the act, but they hauled her into church in the middle of the sermon. You, your church leaders, a crowd of people, and Jesus.

I have no idea of the backstory. Was she a prostitute, and this was a business deal gone wrong? Was it a lust encounter? Did she think she was in love? Was this her first time? Had there been many times? Many men? We just don't know the details, but they really don't matter. Details are not helpful. Who, what, when, and where can actually be unhealthy questions to ask. It does not help the struggler to replay the highlight reel of her lowlights. Nor does it help others to hear the details. In fact, if someone is asking for the details, I am not sure how much they are going to help.

I am not real smart, but even I can see that something is missing in this story. Someone is missing. Where is the guy? Did he jump out the window and get away? Did someone recognize him and let him go? Was he part of a set-up? Was she protecting him?

I know some of what she was feeling, and you may, too. The worst moment of your life is now on display for everyone to know. You are the lead item in the church announcements. Guilt. Shame. Humiliation. Despair. You just want to die. Worst of all, it is your fault. She knew she did it. These were not untrue allegations. There was no speculation or doubt. Consequences of her choices are as bad as they could possibly be, and now she is standing in front of Jesus all by herself.

The Real Agenda

The truth is that the "religious leaders and teachers" did not truly care about the woman. Or the missing man. Their agenda was to destroy Jesus. Let me help you see how this story is meaningful in your situation. It may be that no one will ever know of your sin struggle. It may not be public. For most of you, it will become known. You confess to a few, and the sin of gossip emerges. There is, however, one benefit to a public sin or one that becomes public knowledge. At least you never have to worry about who knows or who might find out. My struggle was quite public. Even today, years later, I am more surprised if someone does not know than if they do.

Even some of your church people will use your sin to further their own agenda. In reality, you are not the issue anyway. Remember the whole "disgrace the cross" discussion? Some will want your sin to negate all your beliefs. Some will want to use it to hurt the church. Some may use it to settle a personal grudge with you.

And some will want to use the knowledge of your sin to make themselves feel better. They loudly condemn in you what they hate in themselves. I have been amazed over time to see so many of the people who condemned me, judged me, and spoke ill of me were hiding their own similar struggles. Some have confessed and asked my forgiveness. Others ended up divorced. Some have left the church. Left Jesus.

Satan wants your sin to embarrass Jesus, so he will do everything he can to stop your repentance. In this story, these men challenged Jesus on the law.

The law instructed them to stone the adulterer. If Jesus extended grace, they'd accuse Him of not respecting Scripture. If He agreed to the stoning, they'd accuse Him of not being loving. Either way, they'd have something to use against Him. Except Jesus wouldn't play their game.

He agreed with the law and invited the one without sin to cast the first stone, which, of course, eliminated everyone—except Him. Then He started writing something in the dirt. When I get to heaven, I am going to ask what He wrote. And I will have plenty of time to get the answer. But I wonder if He wrote...

"I came to save sinners." Maybe He was reminding her that He came to save her. Maybe He was reminding the Pharisees standing there. Maybe even reminding himself. Perhaps indicating they were in the same boat she was in—sinners in need of a Savior.

Maybe it was "I love you." She needed to hear that. So did her accusers. He loved them also.

Or, "Here is a list of your sins." Perhaps He started writing the names of the accusers and listing some of their sins. Maybe put the woman at the top of the list, then the others. But not in a public, humiliating way. Maybe so only they could see it.

You know, I tend to be pretty hard on those so-called teachers. Maybe I do that because of some of my experiences with harsh people. But I really appreciate them at this part of the story. When they figured it out, they stopped. They left, and it was the oldest ones first. Maturity. Spiritual wisdom. They finally got it.

Jesus asked her who was left to condemn her. She said there was no one. Jesus told her He did not condemn her either.

Satan defines you by the humiliation, shame, guilt, and pain of your sin. Jesus defines you by the love, grace, and forgiveness of your sin. He then tells her to go, but to stop sinning. She is to live forgiven. She is not just to confess (even if she was forced into it in some ways). She is to repent. Stop sinning.

So What Is the Point?

You are not condemned. You are forgiven. Live that way. Stop sinning. Live forgiven.

Forgiveness is not just to keep your sins from separating you from God. It is also to enable you to live life in the light.

Never lose sight of how wonderful God has been to you.

My friend Tim doesn't forget.

Great Forgiveness Leads to Great Praise

I have known Tim for over 40 years, and I have watched him fight for his faith and battle his demons for most of those years. Maybe that is why we are friends—we are both faith fighters. You would think it would be easy for him to get discouraged or frustrated at the battle.

But Tim gets the main thing: He is forgiven. He never forgets that. It is what empowers him and energizes him to continue putting one foot in front of the other in his faith journey. Every day.

He is one of the few people I know who exuberantly expresses the joy of his salvation. He's genuinely thankful for the grace of Jesus in his life. He has walked alongside many people on their faith journey. Family members, church friends, college students, me. He is exuberant and joyful in worship. I love sitting near him when praising God because he reminds me of the joy I have in being able to live forgiven.

Tim leads worship and has even led for me countless times when I preach, sings on praise teams, sings at funerals, and teaches Bible classes.

- *He understands what it means to live forgiven.*
- *He gets that God redeems sinners to do kingdom work.*
- *He reminds us all that we must never forget the amazing thing that God has done in removing our sins as far as the east is from the west.*

A Word to the Helpers

Learn to protect one another. Accountability matters for you, too. It works like this. She was a faithful Christian who struggled, and she wanted someone to pray for her. It was between worship and Bible class and I was her "go-to" elder, so she asked for a couple of minutes for prayer. My wife was already on her way to teach Bible class, so we sat down at the back of the auditorium. My friend, Tim, sat down about two rows ahead of us. She began to talk, but she would look at Tim about every other sentence. Finally, she asked if he was there to protect me from her. I said that he was always looking to protect me because that is what brothers do. She knew him and liked him, so he ended up hearing the conversation, too. I didn't signal Tim. I didn't have to. When I saw him notice us, I knew he would come over because we have been watching out for each other for a long time: doing life together with our wives, doing redeemed ministry. He was there just in case, protecting me.

Maybe there is something to remember from our brother, Paul. If he could refer to himself in the present tense as a great sinner, then we aren't "better" than anyone else, including all those we are committed to helping.

In the 16th century, a man named John Bradford saw a group of prisoners and made a statement that is well worth remembering.

"There but for the grace of God go I." There is a small distance between staying in the light and stepping into the darkness. For all the times I took the wrong step, I can also vividly remember the times when I did not—but I easily could have.

Along those lines, be careful about hearing the details. It will not be helpful to them to replay the sin in their minds, and it may not help you.

For those of you whose wounds have turned into scars and are in the battle with those still bleeding as they fight for their faith—you are the living proof that Jesus saves sinners.

Sometimes the best thing my wife and I do for struggling couples is to be a living witness to God's grace, so they can sit and see a couple that made it.

To know what God can do. ■

CHAPTER EIGHT

Forgiveness Is Meant to Be Shared

Forgiveness is hard to receive personally... and it's sometimes hard to accept that others are forgiven. Maybe that is why the Bible says so much about forgiveness. Perhaps one of the reasons this is a hard book to write is that I am trying to reach two different audiences.

One is the struggler fighting for his faith. You need to hear that you are forgiven. Know that truth and accept it.

The other audience is the brother or sister who's trying to help restore the one in need of grace. Often, these audiences overlap. I've been in both of these groups: in need of forgiveness and trying to help others see that they are forgiven, often at the same time.

James wrote a book to Christians that addresses both groups.

Forgiven Faith Life

One of the reasons I love the Book of James is that it's so practical. Like most of us, I need concrete and useful teaching on how to live as a forgiven man of faith. In chapter five of his letter, James ends with some practical advice:

> 13 Is anyone among you suffering? Let him pray. Is anyone
> cheerful? Let him sing praise. 14 Is anyone among you sick? Let
> him call for the elders of the church, and let them pray over
> him, anointing him with oil in the name of the Lord. 15 And the

prayer of faith will save the one who is sick, and the Lord will raise him up. And if he has committed sins, he will be forgiven. [16] Therefore, confess your sins to one another and pray for one another, that you may be healed. The prayer of a righteous person has great power as it is working (James 5:13-16).

If you are in trouble, pray.

If you are happy, sing songs of praise.

If you are sick, get the elders to pray over you and anoint you with oil in the name of the Lord.

I need to say here that growing up I only learned the first two of these. I did not see an anointing until I was serving as an elder, and then I was the one leading it. I did ask a few times about this verse and was always told it was cultural. Just for then and there, not for here and now. Elders could pray and then send you to the doctor. That is what the verse meant. However, that isn't what the verse says. When I became an elder, we started talking about what that verse meant. The elders all agreed we would start doing anointings. We told the congregation and started doing them. There are amazing stories of healing—which should not be a surprise since the Bible says that would happen. Some were not healed physically in the way we asked, but without fail, every single person anointed had a sense of peace about their illness. Even right up until death.

I finally got the connection. It is right there in the passage. If they have sinned, they will be forgiven. There is where the sense of peace comes. You are forgiven. Depending on God, anointing in the name of the Lord—these are acts of faith. You are saved. Forgiven faith living.

We confess our sins and pray for one another, so you may be healed. I am not sure exactly about the cause and effect here, but there is some kind of connection among faith, sin, sickness, and healing. Sin makes you ill. Remember the psalm about how heavily sin weighs on you? It will make you ill until it is resolved. Heart sick. So when you are sick, call the elders to pray and anoint you with oil. Confess your sins and be healed. And when you are confident in your forgiveness, your illness will not be near as frightening. You will be healed.

The prayers of the righteous are powerful.

Healing and forgiveness. They go hand-in-hand.

Sin, Forgiveness, Confession, and Forgetting

My friend, Ed, gets it. We spent about 10 years serving as elders together. He was an outstanding elder: loves people, wants everyone to get to heaven, knows Scripture, and has the courage to act on his convictions. Here is when I knew Ed was a special elder. A couple in trouble reached out for help, so Ed and I went to visit with them. They were wondering if they could make it through an especially difficult time and if they even had a future together. I was just about to share my story when Ed spoke up to tell his story first. He spoke about how he could have lost his marriage during their early years. It wasn't so much because of any one thing he did, but because of neglect. Taking things for granted. Letting their relationship drift until divorce became a possibility.

But Ed's wife would not give up. She said God could heal any and everything. She convinced Ed that God would never give up on their marriage. She told him she would never give up on them, and he should not either. I listened as Ed talked about how his Evy kept loving him until he got his act together. Lots of prayer, lots of working on their God relationship, then working on their relationship. He talked about how in love they were now and how they had a healthy, God-based relationship.

Ed is still modeling a life of faith and forgiveness. His sweet Evy has Alzheimer's. This isn't at all where they thought they would be at this stage of their life. She is now in a care facility. Ed, like every spouse in his situation, wrestles with whether he is doing enough for his mate. He especially hurts when he occasionally loses patience with the situation. Ed talks quite a bit about the fact that Evy never holds it against him. In fact, she does not even remember it.

You already know why Ed tells this story. It's a living reminder of God's grace. God does not hold our sins against us. With His forgiveness, they never occurred.

God forgives and restores.

God does not hold our sins against us.

Ed and Evy are still modeling how to live as forgiven followers. Not like they thought, but still faithful. Still forgiven.

This leads us to the last verse of James 5.

The Point of All This Is...

James ends his letter with a great summary of what confession, repentance, forgiveness, and restoration are really all about:

> 19 My brothers, if anyone among you wanders from the truth and someone brings him back, 20 let him know that whoever brings back a sinner from his wandering will save his soul from death and will cover a multitude of sins (James 5:19-20).

Sometimes we wander from the truth. We meander away from the light. It may not be intentional. Believers do not just wake up one morning and decide to ruin their lives. It happens over time and in a lot of small steps that end up being miles from where—and who—we want to be. You lose focus just like Peter on the water. If you do not keep your heart focused (David), you end up drifting—wandering—from light to the shadows to the darkness.

If you are in a faith fight, there are people who love you and will help bring you back into the light and keep you there. They'll help restore your heart, regain your focus, and walk with you so you stay on track. You can come back no matter where you are or what you have done.

A turn around. That is what we are talking about. Get back on the right road. Change directions. Head the way you want to go. You do need help. It is too hard to do it all by yourself.

Your sin is a sign you are on the wrong road. So change your life direction. Walk back into the light.

The road onto which you have wandered will lead to death if you do not change direction. Walking in the light is a life or death decision that you make every day. Remember, when you come back to the truth of walking in the light, your multitude of sins is covered.

Untreated wounds will kill you. Treated wounds become scars. And all because of. . .

Amazing Grace

It is the most famous hymn ever written and is the most recorded. It's so famous that even when played on bagpipes almost everyone hears the words in their head, which makes it an incredible spiritual experience. It is the words that resonate, not just the music.

John Newton went to sea in his teens and lived about as disreputable a life as possible. In his 20s, he had a religious awakening, which coincided with the time of his life when he was working in the slave trade. Newton went on to became a minister in his 30s and wrote "Amazing Grace" when he was around 50. He also ended up becoming incredibly active in England working to abolish slavery.

Many people think "Amazing Grace" was written as a song of penance for his work in the slave trade. It was so much more than that, even though the horror, shame, and guilt of what he did as a slaver stayed with him all his life. "Amazing Grace" was a song about all his life of sin: alcohol, debauchery, and rebellion.

When John Newton wrote "Amazing Grace," it was personal. It was his story. He wrote it to illustrate a sermon, and it turned into something to illustrate his life, and for many of us... our life.

It is personal to me when I sing it because I get the whole "that saved a wretch like me."

I understand "was blind and now I see."

I cry at "I once was lost but now am found."

You do too. It is especially meaningful for those of us who know Jesus yet have had to struggle for our faith. It is significant for those who find Jesus. It is meaningful for those who fight to stay in Jesus.

Amazing grace is a sweet sound. To know that your sins have been forgiven by God. Never to be held against you. God has saved us. In spite of who we are and what we have done.

Amazing Grace!

Grace that is forever mine.

Grace that will lead me home.

A Word to the Helpers

Ed and Evy is a great story about how it is possible to change your spiritual journey, to walk more in the light, to focus your heart. It is also a reminder of the power of our stories. God did not just redeem Ed's story; He made it into a powerful testimony to help others.

I watched that couple listen to Ed. I saw them realizing he was modeling confession, repentance, forgiveness, and restoration. There is power in our stories of redemption. There is power in seeing someone who made it. Not just made it through a wilderness, but is thriving. If they can... you can.

You know people who need someone to help bring them back into the light. That someone might be you. It may happen because a struggler realizes how wounded they are and seeks your help. Maybe you realize one of your brothers or sisters is struggling, and you reach out to them. We are in this together.

For those of you on the front lines of recapturing wandering sinners for Jesus... you are engaged in a life and death struggle. What you are doing to help does have eternal consequences. It matters.

Because of your love and faithfulness, because of your hard work, and because of your willingness to do the messy work of life with strugglers—there are going to be people in heaven who may not have made it if you had not helped them back onto the road of light and people who might have died. ■

The Goal Is to Restore

I am not writing this book because I repented of my sins, though I absolutely have. I am not writing this book because God has forgiven me, though He has certainly done that. I am writing this book because I have been restored. I have been made like I was before the struggle. Understand that restoration cannot happen without confession, repentance, and forgiveness. The ultimate goal is for the struggling sinner to be an active and valued member of their community of faith. I struggled with my sins for a long time, as have many of you, but you can overcome your struggles. I have preached a lot of years, served many years as an elder, all because of restoration—a spiritual "bringing back."

So let's start with some reminders to those of you committed to help bring the strugglers into the light.

A Word to the Helpers

> 1 Brothers, if anyone is caught in any transgression, you who are spiritual should restore him in a spirit of gentleness. Keep watch on yourself, lest you too be tempted. 2 Bear one another's burdens, and so fulfill the law of Christ (Galatians 6:1-2).

Spiritual people have an obligation to those trapped in their sin. This is no time for false modesty. You know if you are a spiritual person or not. This certainly applies to elders and their wives. But also, preachers, members, those in the church who are spiritual leaders. Often, these are the very people who have seen their wounds turn into scars. Because spiritual people helped them. There will be people you assume are spiritual who will not be helpful. They will be judgmental and harsh. They're the ones who will think you deserve whatever consequences come your way, so they will not help you deal with them.

For those of you committed to helping our struggling brothers and sisters... the goal is to restore them. Bring them back into the light, bring them home, welcome them back. There are two reminders for those committed to the work of restoration.

Be gentle. Firm when needed, but always gentle. You are dealing with people who are in trouble. The time will come when you will want to give up on them. You may sometimes want to snap at them, rip into them. Their struggles can make you mad, aggravated, disgusted, and sick. Sometimes they will say hard things to you:

- *Who are you to tell me what to do?*
- *You can't judge me.*
- *You don't love me.*
- *There are people worse than me you should be helping.*
- *I don't want your help.*

But remember that you are helping people whose spiritual self-esteem is low. Their intense sense of failure will sometimes lead to an effort to push away the people trying to help. If we react harshly, we just reinforce to them that they are unworthy of help.

Be gentle with the wounded brother.

And do not get caught up in their sin. Be careful in dealing with strugglers who share your areas of temptation. That is just one reason I am not a supporter of solo spiritual counseling. It's too dangerous, even for the spiritual among us. Do not work alone.

Here is a helpful way to remember this:

- *Don't let the alcoholic prepare the communion wine by himself.*
- *Don't let the thief count the contribution by himself.*
- *Don't let the adulterer do marriage counseling by himself.*

Yes, by the grace of God we are changed. Just always be aware of how, when, and where you are vulnerable.

Wounds into scars.

Just be careful never to put yourself in a position to turn your scars back into wounds. ■

CHAPTER NINE

What Do You Want to Happen?

It is critical that the struggling sinner decides what he wants to happen in his life. It's also critical that those of us helping decide what we want to happen. Generally, the struggler and the helper all want the same thing—restoration. Maybe that is why we need to start with the story of...

The Most Famous Prodigal of All

In fact, it's his story that gives us the term "prodigal son." You can read the story on your own—and you should—in Luke 15. It's the most obvious story to review when restoration is your ultimate goal.

The problem started because the younger son in this story lost his heart focus. Life became about pleasing himself, not God. He didn't think about his father. He thought about the world. When he left his family and traveled afar, he was also leaving his support system. It's hard to do this life alone, especially when trouble comes. While he was away, he spent his inheritance in wild living. He fed his worldly appetite.

Then the hard times came, just like they always do. It was a famine. He could not even meet his basic needs. He had no community around him. He had no emotional, financial, or spiritual resources. He was lonely, hungry, and desperate.

The young man was desperate enough to take a job feeding

pigs. Slopping hogs. I've done that. It's nasty, filthy, disgusting, hard, messy, smelly work. He was desperate enough that he would have eaten what he was feeding to the hogs. No one was there to help him because he had false friends when he needed faith friends.

It Was a Wake-Up Call

He came to his senses. You may be reading this book because you have come to your senses. Maybe because you were caught. Maybe you woke up one day and realized you did not even know how you got to this point in your life, but you are tired of it. Maybe you are starting to realize what you are losing or what you have already lost. Your wake-up call could have been an alcohol-fueled wreck, your spouse serving you divorce papers, a close call, an arrest, or a confrontation by someone who really loves you. The young man in this story had his wake-up call when he lost everything.

But he did something about it. He resolved to confess his sins. He even rehearsed his speech. He devised a plan and acted on it. He got up and got started on the journey home. It may be that time for you. Maybe it's time to find someone you trust to help you go home: your mate, an elder couple, a preacher and wife, parents, or a friend/s. If you are not sure who will help, look for the people with scars. They have been there and found their way home. They know the way back.

As the prodigal neared home, his father saw him and ran to welcome him home. He was looking for him. God is longing for you to come home. There are people who love you and want you to return to the light. And a word to the church—we have to be looking for, searching for, longing for our prodigals to come home. Run to them. Meet them to walk alongside them as they come home. Go with them to see their mate, their parent, their church. Be there.

Because Confession Matters

Listen to the confession of the prodigal. He sounds just like David acknowledging his sin against Bathsheba. *I have sinned against heaven and you.* That was the confession. My sin has hurt God, and it has hurt you. He even acknowledges that he is not worthy to be called his father's son, and that is truth. Prodigals know how unworthy we are. Prodigals that left for the far away country. Prodigals that stayed but had heart struggles. They know what they did, and they know the pain they caused. They know they are not worthy. But of course, truth be told (and it is), none of us are worthy.

So let the party begin. The father threw a coming home party for his prodigal son because the son that was dead is alive. The son who was lost is now found.

But Know That Some Will Not

There is always an older brother who gets angry and will not come to the party because he was the "good" son. You know, the one who stayed behind and "slaved" for Dad. The one who never disobeyed, at least not outwardly. The son who wasted everything on prostitutes comes back and gets a party, but the good son never got his party. Of course, he was wrong. Wrong in so many ways.

He, too, was a prodigal. Maybe not outwardly, but certainly inwardly. He just didn't know it or wouldn't admit it. Was he jealous? Did he wish he could have gone away and partied like his little brother? He is hiding his own heart issues. I "slaved" for you does not sound like a loving son. Was he mad that the prodigal "got away with it?" The prodigal didn't get away with anything. The pain, the wasted years, the hurt he caused—all these things were always right in front of him.

The father has to remind the older brother that all he has left belongs to his oldest son. The younger brother already had his inheritance and spent it all. There were consequences, but let's celebrate. Your dead brother is alive. Your lost brother is found.

And Sometimes Sinners Make the Wrong Choice

He had a long history of sexual misconduct with young minors. He was convicted in a court of law twice. Numerous other situations could also be confirmed. He was currently out on parole, registered as a sex offender, and he called one of our elders about coming to church.

I have to be honest here. Consequences for sin are sometimes hard. Our elders had lots of long, intense meetings. Lots of prayers, tears, even anger. Opinions ran the gamut of emotions as you would expect.

- *"We can't sit in judgment."*
- *"You cannot put conditions on repentance."*
- *"We must not endanger our children."*
- *"We have to protect the flock."*

Well, you get the idea. So, a group of us came up with a list of talking points to get clarity on how to shepherd both this man and our flock. Two points were agreed on immediately: God can forgive anything, and the ultimate goal was restoration.

We also identified a number of problems. He had a long track record of sin. He had no track record of change and repentance. He would not confess to any sin, even the public convictions. We agreed that our flock had to be protected.

We came up with what we prayed would be a workable plan for restoration. He would not be allowed on church grounds unless accompanied by an elder. He could not go anywhere near the children's wing in the building. The church would have to be informed in some way and to some extent. At that time, we were having an evening service with an attendance of about 40 members, the majority of whom were over 70 years old. He would only be allowed to attend that service. He could not contact any members on his own initiative. He could not attend any church activities outside of worship.

He was furious when we asked to meet and discuss the conditions of his attending worship and outlined this plan. He insisted we had to accept him as a full member with no conditions.

We communicated that his attitude seemed far short of confession and repentance.

He said he would just go elsewhere.

We told him we would have to communicate these discussions with any church he decided to attend. That actually did happen twice. We found out he was attending a different congregation and we called to discuss it. At one church, he told them he had never been convicted of anything. At the other, he told them we had said he would never be welcome under any circumstances. He was still lying.

Sometimes you do the best you can to welcome home the prodigal, and sometimes they still make the wrong choice.

And Sometimes They Just Don't Get It

He is one of the most reviled men in history. The betrayer. The one who sold Jesus out—Judas.

Even before he betrays Jesus, he was living on the edge of the light and struggling with his heart. He used to help himself to the moneybag. I don't know how much, and I do not know why. Was he losing too much money betting on the camel races? Did he have a fondness for designer sandals? Was there family pressure? Did he resent the simple lifestyle embraced by Jesus? Did he think his job or the ministry he was doing entitled him to it? Did he intend to pay it back?

The truth is that we do not know much about what got Judas started down the wrong road. He was evidently still doing ministry with Jesus and the other disciples, but he was in trouble. Maybe he saw the 30 pieces of silver as the answer to all his problems. Remember the "things of the world" that we cannot love? Greed is one of them. Wanting things you do not have. Lusting after money.

And it led him to sell out Jesus.

But here is what we sometimes forget; Judas confessed.

"I have sinned by betraying innocent blood" (Matthew 27:4).

Sin. Confession. Repentance. Forgiveness. Restoration.

Judas confessed his sin. He started working on repenting. Returned the 30 pieces of silver and was clearly headed back into the light, believing in Jesus... until he killed himself.

Somehow Judas did not get it. He did not understand. Did he not think he could be forgiven? Did the shame and guilt overwhelm him to the point that he did not think anyone would understand? Did he not remember the story of David? Didn't he hear the story of the Prodigal Son? Had he forgotten the woman caught in adultery? Did he not understand that he could be restored?

My personal conviction is that Judas could have proclaimed Jesus for the rest of his days. Just like Peter did. Where were the voices that could have, even should have, helped him envision a different future?

If you find yourself wondering if you can be forgiven, if you can be restored, if you have a future... then learn these lessons that Judas never did. Please understand what he did not.

Forgiveness is real. Restoration is possible. Hear love, grace, mercy, forgiveness. Do not listen to guilt, shame, and humiliation.

I am not naïve, and you should not be either. I know about the older brother syndrome. There would have been those that always labeled Judas by his sin. Those that would never forgive him or accept him. I want to believe that Peter, John, Mary, or Thomas would have walked beside him on the redemption road.

Forgiveness is real, and restoration is possible.

Believe that and live that because our wounds that have turned into scars are the living witness to this truth.

Thank You, God.

A Word to the Helpers

You don't always know when it's going to happen. That moment when someone comes to their senses. The time when they are ready to come back into the light and stay there. If you are committed to helping people, you must decide how you'll treat the prodigal who decides to come home. Be ready for when that moment happens in their life.

Early in my ministry career, we found out someone in our youth group was planning to bring pot on an upcoming retreat. I confronted him, and he admitted it—and admitted he had a pretty serious problem. We met with his parents, and that's when I learned the difference between the Father's love and the older brother syndrome. As soon as I explained what the meeting was about, the dad exploded. He pushed his son against the wall and began yelling at him. His mom began to cry and kept asking how he could do that to them.

Fortunately, my Dad—who was a really good elder and was in on the meeting—was there to help defuse the situation.

Here is what I learned. Those parents actually cared, but they handled a bad situation in the worst possible way, doing exactly the wrong things. Yes, their son had issues, but they made it worse, gave him an excuse to not work on the issue, and raised barriers to his coming back into the light.

If you want to help someone, you must be in control of your emotions. Express emotion, but control it. After all, the situation isn't about you. Your anger must stay righteous. Of course, there may be damage control for the consequences, but stay focused.

We are bringing hearts back into the light, and we want them to stay in the light.

Because Compassion Matters

Our hearts must hurt for the wounded. That is why the scarred people get it. We have been there. We know what you are going through. We remember the pain. Our prodigals must feel our love and compassion: hug them, eat with them, sit by them at church, show up in court, listen, speak truth into their lives, speak in love.

So What Kind of Church Are You Going to Be?

If your community of faith is an "older brother" church, then stop and repent. Change your church culture. Your church is full of prodigals. Maybe it is time to be honest about it. Do not put barriers up that discourage the prodigal from coming home. That is not the heart of Jesus. When you do that, you are drifting from the light.

- *Be the church where the messed up come to get better.*
- *Be a church that celebrates the prodigals who come home.*
- *Be a church where wounds become scars.*

Time for a Hard Truth

> Though they know God's righteous decree that those who practice such things deserve to die, they not only do them but give approval to those who practice them (Romans 1:32).

It may be time to say something else directly to those committed to helping the struggler battling his or her sin. Sometimes confrontation has to happen, and sometimes it is ugly. Sometimes they get caught, and you must confront them in love. You are not sure how they will react. It is hard because you found out and know you should reach out. Hard because you are not sure what they really want to do. Truth is not always well-received. It is tough emotionally to have to confront someone with their sin. It's tough on them and tough on you.

It's sometimes tempting to take the easy way out. It's easy not to confront anyone. It's easy not to speak truth. It's easy to go along with the lies Satan is telling. He tells them lies about why their sin isn't so bad. He lies to you about it being none of your business.

Some people resist repentance. Some will try to justify—excuse their actions. Some are just not willing to end their sinful behavior.

Some will turn on you. They'll call you unloving, judgmental, hypocritical. They will not only want you to leave them alone, but they'll also even want you to endorse their behavior.

Remember these three things:

1. *There are behaviors that God says should result in death.*
2. *The goal is not to get them "back in church." The goal is to help them out of the darkness and back into the light. It is a heart issue.*
3. *Repentance and confession lead to forgiveness and restoration.*

Resist the temptation to approve or endorse their behavior. It's easier to do almost anything other than confront a brother or sister in sin. It's definitely easier to just ignore it and let them die in sin. I mean, isn't it their choice anyway? It's much easier to endorse their behavior. After all, maybe we do not really understand what God meant about sin and death, or maybe God did not really mean it. And on and on the excuses go. But these behaviors do not save a soul from death and cover a multitude of sins.

Do the hard thing. Confront the sinner in love, and do it gently, but do it with truth. Walk with them into the light. Spend the time, energy, effort, and money to help them.

It's a matter of life and death.

If you want to help a Christian caught in sin, speak truth. Do not compromise. Be gentle. Be loving. Be faithful.

If you are the one caught in a sin, those coming to you do not have a choice. If they ignore your sin, they tacitly approve it. They love God enough, and they love you enough, to help you get out of darkness and back into light. So they will be firm about what God says. You also have a choice about what to do.

A Last Thought About Judas

For those of us committed to helping restore the struggler . . . how would we have treated Judas? Would he be welcome in our church? In our small group? In our home?

There are still people like Judas among us.

Do they see Jesus in how we treat them? ■

CHAPTER TEN

Restoration Really Does Happen

It was a hard time for me. Determined to defeat my demons once and for all, I had confessed, resigned my ministry position, and was doing the hard work of repentance. I decided that to be the person God wanted, I would step away from full-time ministry. I had no job and was moving away from the only career I had ever known.

One night, Tony called. And he called the next night. For several months, he called every night around 11:00. We were friends and preaching buddies. Our boys played ball together, and I had a lot of respect for Tony. He had heard about what was going on and wanted to be there.

He called every night. The calls were short. He often read a verse to me about forgiveness and reminded me that God still had great things to do through me and with me. Then he prayed over me.

Even though I have told him many times, I don't think Tony knows to this day how much those two-minute phone calls meant to me: knowing he believed I still had value, Scripture, encouragement, and prayer. He does not even clearly remember doing that for me. That's when it dawned on me that he probably had done that same thing for dozens and dozens of struggling believers.

Forgiveness and restoration really can—and do—happen. Thank you, Tony, for reminding me that God was with me and was not through with me.

God used Tony to help me remember that God is a God of restoration *and* forgiveness—not just forgiveness.

Just Ask Peter

I have talked a lot about Peter in this book. I teach and preach a lot from the life of Peter. He's one of my favorite characters in all the Bible. A sinful man who is awed by the power of Jesus. A man of great faith who walked on the water. Till he went under. And was pulled up by Jesus (restored) to walk again on the water. The man who attacked the High Priest himself in defense of Jesus.

And the one who denied Jesus.

Three times.

He was warned. Jesus told His closest followers that they would fall away. Satan would, of course, come after them. Remember the whole roaring lion thing? They would lose focus and forget to guard their hearts. Happens to us.

Not Peter! Never! He was adamant and vocal about it. Here is the thing to know about Peter. He meant it. He was not arrogantly boasting about what he knew was not true. I think he believed with every fiber of his being that he would never fall away from Jesus. Never leave the light. Not even for a second. He serves as a reminder that we all have be careful. We have to be continually on guard, or we will fall.

Jesus told him that yes, he would fall away. Peter said he would not. By the way, the rest of the apostles were saying it and believing it also. But maybe Peter was the loudest. Jesus told him he would deny Him three times before the rooster crows.

Peter and some of the others followed Jesus into the Garden where Jesus prayed. Peter couldn't stay awake. They were spiritually, mentally, emotionally, and physically exhausted. Tiredness is one of the triggers we have talked about. Peter was vulnerable and didn't even realize it.

When they went to arrest Jesus, Peter leaped to His defense and attacked the High Priest. The servant of the High Priest got between them, and Peter cut off his ear. I imagine Peter expected to die right then and there defending his Lord... until Jesus stopped him and even replaced the ear. Peter had it all wrong because he didn't understand. He was tired, embarrassed, and confused.

But even then—even when most of the other disciples were running for their lives—Peter still followed Jesus all the way into the courtyard. That is faith. Then he had three different chances to confess that faith to acknowledge that he knew Jesus and was one of His followers. One witness identified him, another pointed out his accent. He was asked point blank. Each time, he denied, denied, and denied. Even with curses, he denied Jesus.

Then the rooster crowed. And Jesus looked right at him.

That is when he realized what he had done. He was shattered. Peter wept bitterly. Ashamed. Guilty. Broken.

I believe there was something in the look of Jesus that called to him. It wasn't scornful or accusatory. Not condemnation. Not guilt. Not shame. My opinion? I think Peter saw love in the eyes of Jesus. Sorrow and pain, but pain for Peter. That may have been what hurt Peter the most. It may also have been what called him back and brought him to his senses and made him move back into the light.

Christians who truly love God sometimes disappoint Him. It breaks God's heart, but it breaks their hearts, too. Maybe you've been there. I have. I've been sorry, and I have been broken.

Fast forward to the days after the resurrection. Jesus and Peter had another conversation at which time Jesus asked Peter, "Do you love me? "Lord, you know I love you."

Three times He asked, and Peter answered three times until his feelings were hurt. Because he really did love Jesus. He knew that Jesus knew it, too. Then Jesus told Peter to feed his sheep. He was going to entrust His flock to Peter. There would still be a mission for Peter. His wounds becoming scars.

The Pentecost sermon, jail, leading people to Jesus, healing, loving, and following Jesus.

Jesus also predicted the way Peter would die. Martyred.

He was crucified for his faith. When they got ready to execute him, tradition says that Peter asked to be crucified upside down because he was not worthy to die like his Lord.

Great faith. Great failure. Great faith. Repeat. But always ending in great faith.

God used Peter in powerful ways.

Sin, confession, repentance, forgiveness, restoration.

Wounds into scars.

Just Ask Dr. Bobby

In his own words, "I woke up one morning, looked out the window, and thought... *How did I get here? This is not who I am."*

It started out so well. A college athlete, med school, a successful practice, wife and kids, strong faith, active in church, and a leader in church. But lots of pressure professionally. Having to deal with other people's sin that spilled over onto him. Eventually his marriage fell apart.

Remember "**HALT**": **h**ungry, **a**ngry, **l**onely, **t**ired. You get really vulnerable. Satan tempts you, and sin happens. You repent and confess, but the enemy keeps attacking.

The cycle continues until the faithful Christian wakes up one day and realizes they are not living consistent with their faith. Just like the Prodigal Son who came to his senses.

That is what Bobby did. He came to accept that he could not control what anyone else did, but he could control what he did. He went to work on his heart. Confessed his sin. Worked on being a good dad. Met and married a faithful Christian woman.

Now he works as an emergency room doctor. He uses his income to support a number of missionaries. He's made dozens and dozens of preaching trips overseas at his own expense. In fact, he and wife go on several mission trips every year. He is chairman of the mission committee at his church. He gives a lot of counsel and advice to hurting people. Lots of people have come to know Jesus because he came to his senses and decided to live true to his heart:

- *Badly wounded by his own sin and the sins of others.*
- *Confessed and centered his heart in the light.*
- *Worked on managing consequences from his sin.*
- *Learned to stay alert and focused.*
- *Watched his wounds turn into scars.*

He continues to bring people to Jesus, helping others realize their sin is not the end of their story:

- *Forgiven*
- *Restored*
- *Making a difference*

And Ask David

We have looked at length at David's sin with Bathsheba, but we also need to spend some time with Psalm 51. This is David's prayer to God after his sin. It is perhaps the clearest description of sin, confession, repentance, forgiveness, and restoration. And it may be the most famous.

This can also serve as your restoration blueprint. It is the story you want to write when your wounds have become scars.

Here are the highlights that will remind you of many of the things we have discussed so far:

Verses 1-2 Here is David's plea for God's mercy, love, and forgiveness. It is an appeal for God to blot out his transgressions—wash him from his iniquity—cleanse him from his sin. That is what we sinners really want:ot be forgiven so completely that our sins are no longer even a faint stain on our lives.

Verses 3-5 Confession. He knows what he has done. In fact, his sin is always before him. His sin is against God above anyone else. It's as if he was born in sin. David recognizes the real issue is a God—heart problem. He needed to "return to the light." This is the darkest part of David's prayer, and I get it. The memory, the shame, the guilt, and the fact of your sin are constantly on your mind.

Verses 6-7 David knows what God desires. God wants his heart. God wants truth to be a part of his very being. Not something just believed, but lived. Praying for wisdom so he is equipped to do better. Claiming God's total forgiveness. You make me clean. Clean, not dirt removal but still leaving a stain, but clean! God has washed him whiter than snow. Pure again. As if he had never sinned. Forgiveness.

Verses 8-9 David's desire is for joy and gladness to be heard in his life again. Forgiveness and restoration. He is broken and begs God not to hide His face from him, but to blot out his iniquities. Forgiveness, complete and total forgiveness, is what we all desire. To not just be forgiven, but to feel forgiven.

Verses 10-11 He asks God to create a clean heart in him. There it is again. Sin is a heart issue. David wants to deal with the issue. He wants God to renew a right spirit in him. That is the beginning of restoration. Do not cast me away. He is pleading for value and for spiritual self-worth. Do not take away your Holy Spirit. Let it not be too late. I want you to know that if you're reading this and feeling your heart turning back to God, it isn't too late for you. It wasn't too late for David. Or Dr. Bobby. Or me.

Verses 12-13 Restore the joy of your salvation. Be happy despite your sin because God has wiped it away. Party like the Prodigal Son. Lost and now found. Dead and now alive.

Then David pledges to teach sinners the way of God. Purpose. Healed so you can heal others. David knows sinners will return to God. A multitude of sins will be covered. Bringing back sinners. Restore me, and use me to restore others.

Verses 14-15 Deliver me from blood guilt, and my forgiven tongue will sing aloud of righteousness and my mouth will declare your praise. Forgiven sinners get it. It is why my friend Tim is joyous in praise. It is why I am. To tell the truth, it is why I talk so much about God and Jesus. Like David, I have an amazing story of forgiveness. So praise God for what He has done in forgiving you. Declare it. Be a witness to God's grace. Testify to His mercy. You are living proof.

Verses 16-17 But it is not going to just be about actions. God does not just want sacrifices and offerings. That would be easy to do. God wants a broken spirit and a broken and contrite heart. David knew it, and I know it. Because when you are broken, God can heal:

- *Broken to confess and repent*
- *To be forgiven and restored*
- *To be used to help others come back to Jesus*
- *Wounds into scars*

You Can Even Ask Joshua

I know I have read through the Minor Prophets several times in the past, so I am not sure how this story never grabbed my attention until a few years ago. It is in Zechariah 3, and it is a story of sin, forgiveness, and restoration.

We are getting a glimpse of the judgment seat of God, and Joshua the High Priest is standing there. God, angels, a leader of God's people (Joshua)... and Satan. The devil is there to accuse Joshua.

There it is. The thing we are all afraid of deep down. Our sin will catch up to us. We will stand before the throne of God, and Satan will be there to accuse us. There is so much sin for Satan to work with, and he does not even have to lie about me. I have done things I shouldn't have done. I did not do things I should have done. I certainly don't want Satan standing at the judgement to give a play-by-play of my life failures.

But the Lord rebukes Satan. Because of Jesus, we do not have to fear the Judgment Day. Satan will not even be allowed to open his mouth against us.

God says that Joshua is a "stick snatched from the burning fire." That sure describes me. Maybe it describes you, too. We were being consumed by fire on our way to hell. Jesus and God snatched me from the fire. Just like He did some of you. Just like He can do for any of you reading this. Reach for Jesus. Just like Peter did when he was drowning or burning or dead or lost. Now saved. Snatched from the fire.

Joshua was wearing filthy clothes. That is what our life often looks like in the aftermath of our sin. What a mess we have made! What a mess Joshua must have made of his life! But his filthy clothes are removed and replaced with clean ones.

"I have taken away your sin."

Forgiveness. Filthy clothes replaced with rich clothes and a clean head covering.

Joshua was given a charge. He was told to walk in the ways of God and to keep His requirements. Much like returning to the light. And staying there. Like the woman caught in adultery—go and quit your life of sin. Repentance.

Joshua was given responsibility. Govern my house and have charge of my courts. You will lead my people. It was real restoration. Joshua was promised a place among those standing around the throne of God. Heaven. Saved.

Then in verse 10, we read the reminder that under Joshua's compassionate, confident leadership, people will invite neighbors to sit in their garden—bringing others into the kingdom to join us in living forgiven.

God is turning your wounds into scars. He is restoring you to do kingdom work: helping the walking wounded, restoring the prodigal, inviting others into the kingdom.

You are being snatched out of the fire so that God can do something beautiful in you and through you.

A Word to the Helpers

Remember that Satan came after Jesus. If Satan tried to cause Jesus to sin, he certainly will try to cause you to sin. Perhaps this is the place to remind you about Jesus, temptation... and you. There are both lessons and reminders for those you are helping in this story.

The story is found in Matthew 4:1-11.

In many ways, it is a review of what you've read throughout this book. Jesus was led into the wilderness by the Holy Spirit to be tempted by the devil. It was not as if Jesus was going to succumb to the pressure of Satan. He knew it, the Holy Spirit knew it, and I suspect Satan knew it. Regardless, He had to experience life just as we do, and that meant being tempted so He would understand what we experience. And so He could show us how to battle Satan. To be ready for the battle, Jesus spent 40 days fasting in preparation.

We will be tempted by Satan, the roaring lion that wants to devour us. So be ready and stay focused. Keep our hearts on point and stay in the light. Take care of yourself so you can help others. Stay prepared.

Satan tried three specific temptations with Jesus. They are the things of the world that we cannot love.

He turned stones into bread after 40 days of Jesus' fasting. Make no mistake, Jesus could have turned those stones into bread. When we encounter a physical temptation, Jesus gets it. He was as hungry for food as we will ever be for anything. He knows how it is to hunger for something.

Satan continued to mock Jesus: *Jump off the temple, and make the angels catch you.* There is the pride and ego at work. *Prove you are the Son of God.* When we are tempted to exert our ego and pride, Jesus understands. When you want to "prove" something, Jesus gets it.

Look out, and know that Satan will give you everything you see. Greed. Wanting things. Wanting things so bad you will do anything to get them. Jesus gets it.

It is so comforting to me to know that Jesus understands exactly how I feel when I have to battle my demons. It is comforting to you and to those you are helping.

So how did Jesus resist?

- **He used Scripture.** *Jesus used God's Word against Satan. Here are some things we need to learn from how Jesus dealt with temptation.*
- **Live on God's Word.** *Read it. Study it. Memorize it. Use it. Know it.*
- **Do not put God to the test.** *God is not your personal 911 call only to be used in emergencies. Or just when you need—or want—something.*
- **Only worship God.** *Keep your heart focused. Remember that sin is ultimately against God. That is the core of our sin struggle. Let God stay in control.*

The devil left Jesus after this. Clearly Satan is a sore loser. When you resist Satan, he will run. There is always a way out.

Then the angels came and took care of Jesus. No one has to fight this battle alone.

Our helpers are making sure of that. ■

A Few Last Words for the Helpers

If you are going to help the struggler come back into the light—and stay there—it is a marathon, not a sprint. It takes time, energy, and effort. There will be times where you will wonder what else you can say to them, what other resources you can offer. I thought it might be helpful to remind you of the concepts—the beliefs—I come back to time and time again in giving counsel and advice. Often, we will meet with someone several times over a period of weeks or months. Not just while they are working through the initial decision to repent and confess, but after they are back in the light. It is a process to help them get a strong start down the right road. We discuss one of these concepts with them, have them work with it for a week or two, and then move to the next one, but I want to start off with another story.

When they came to see to see us, their marriage was in crisis, but they were willing to talk to us. A friend had referred them and even set up the initial contact. Now this couple sat in our living room at opposite ends of the couch. They shared their story of drifting apart, crossing lines, not really wanting to be where they were but not sure what to do about it.

In looking for something of a starting point, I asked if they loved each other.

"Not now."

"No, I do not."

Now what? I was a little at a loss for where to go next when my wife asked a question to each of them.

"Do you love God?"

They both answered that they still loved God, so that is where we started. We visited about repentance, confession, and what it meant to live that out in view of loving God. We coached them both about receiving and extending forgiveness and how to live that out. We talked about what God would want and what it meant to love Him in a wrecked marriage. We also discussed what reconciliation looked like based on the foundation of loving God, read a lot of Scripture, and prayed a lot of prayers.

As they began to reconcile, we moved into talking about how to maintain focus; helped set up plans, boundaries, and parameters for their relationship—preventive medicine so to speak. All based on the foundation of loving God with all you are.

They fell back in love. It has been over a decade, and they are still faithful and active in their church today. Still active leaders in the youth program. Still married. Still living their forgiveness.

And it started with re-digging their foundations. Going back to the basics.

Here are six foundational concepts to share and utilize as you help strugglers strengthen their walk in the light.

1. The Greatest Command Love God with everything you have. Most people you are helping know this, but it is a great daily reminder. What does today look like if I make "loving God" choices all day? What does that look like in my marriage? How does that speak to my addictions? Memorizing it from Mark 12:30, singing it, praying about it. It helps keep both you and the one you are helping to stay focused and to keep your heart true. It is a practical and concrete resource.

2. And The Second Love everyone as you do yourself. Mark 12:31. There are several practical advantages to using this verse as a resource. It takes the focus off what is happening to them and encourages them to look outside themselves. Wrestle with what it means to love yourself in the context of loving God. How does that affect relationships? How do you maintain a healthy spiritual ego? Hint: Love God and love others. Encourage them to think about this verse. Talk with them about what it means to live like this. Memorize it. Both of these first two concepts are great filters for every decision. Even as you help them work through consequences and how to handle them, use these as the framework.

3. Remember Your Baptism There are so many great verses to learn and reflect on, but I encourage you to use Romans 6:3-5. After all, Paul is reminding the Christians in Rome about what their baptism really means. It lets you talk with them about dying with Christ and being raised to a new life. The rest of chapter 6 has quite a bit to say about the choice between sin and Jesus. It's even helpful to remember how clean they felt coming out of the baptism water. God's forgiveness allows them to have that same feeling. Colossians 2:12 through chapter 3 is excellent to read and study. It serves as a reminder and a blueprint of how to live out their baptism.

These first three are more about re-digging your foundations, while these next three are useful in reminding them that there are living and active resources to help them on their journey.

4. The Bible Use your Bible to help stay focused. After all, Jesus used it when He was tempted, so it's obviously a tool to help defeat Satan. In spiritual warfare, you need truth, not opinion. You don't need to guess at what sin is or to simply have an opinion that you are fine or to have false hope. You must be certain.

For those of you who are helpers, using Scripture does two things: It grounds your spiritual counseling in truth, and it keeps your counsel from being taken as some kind of personal attack. If they don't like what's being said, let them argue with God, not you.

Many strugglers are familiar with the Bible. Some are even teachers of it. For most of us, studying Scripture isn't about learning what to do or not do. It's about putting knowledge into practice, but we need to be reminded of what we know. Crisis has a way of sharpening our focus so that we hear clearer. We study so that truth is in us so that it's there when we need it to resist the devil:

> [16] All Scripture is breathed out by God and profitable for teaching, for reproof, for correction, and for training in righteousness, [17] that the man of God may be complete, equipped for every good work (2 Timothy 3:16-17).

5. The Holy Spirit Sometimes we will just work through Romans 8 with those we counsel. They need to know how powerful the Holy Spirit is. It's good to remind them—or teach them—that...

- *The Holy Spirit lives in us.*
- *The Holy Spirit gives us life.*
- *The Holy Spirit puts to death wrong deeds.*
- *The Holy Spirit helps us pray.*

6. Community of faith You have a community of faith that will help you. Those you work with need one, too. It is too hard to do this alone, so God uses other people to help. Nathan with David, Andrew with Peter, Tony with me, me with Stephen. You get the idea.

> [9] Two are better than one, because they have a good reward for their toil. [10] For if they fall, one will lift up his fellow. But woe to him who is alone when he falls and has not another to lift him up! [11] Again, if two lie together, they keep warm, but how can one keep warm alone? [12] And though a man might prevail against one who is alone, two will withstand him—a threefold cord is not quickly broken (Ecclesiastes 4:9-12).

If one falls down—this is exactly where the struggler finds himself—you can help him up. There are people to do church life with who are committed to helping the fallen because a cord of three strands is not easily broken. The struggler, you the helpers, and our God.

Helpers may be a mate, a friend, an elder, someone in their small group, or maybe someone whose wounds are now scars. People who will pray, walk beside, and speak truth. That is the task of those committed to helping and healing.

Here are some of the times the struggler needs help from his community:

- *When they are caught in sin and need spiritual helpers to restore them, they need someone to intervene and speak truth. It may be when they come to their senses and need to confess. It may be when they need help coming back into the light.*
- *It may be when they are losing focus and need people who love them to ask hard questions and give advice.*
- *When the "older brother" attacks, they need someone to protect and defend them.*
- *When struggling with consequences and about to be overwhelmed. When they hurt over their sin and need encouragement. When they are trying to get their life together and cannot quite find their way.*

This is what spiritual people in a community of faith do for a struggler to help them stay in the light.

- **PRAY** *For forgiveness, but also for restoration and protection.*
- **LISTEN** *Sometimes strugglers need to express pain and hurt. They will need to talk about the guilt they feel with safe people who love them.*
- **SPEAK TRUTH** *Even when they do not always want to hear it. Or to speak forgiveness, grace, and restoration into their life.*
- **SHOW UP** *They need people to be there, to offer meals and activities., and even to sit with them at church.*

My wife and I will often invite additional people into the conversation at this point. We seek to be living proof that there really is a church family committed to walking alongside them. Sometimes we ask those we are helping to identify who it is they want to walk with them. Sometimes we select the other helpers. The important thing is to use the resource that a faith community provides.

Use these resourses as helpful ways to enable your restored brother or sister to stay on track, stay focused, and continue walking in the light. ■

Conclusion: Faith Fighters

It is always difficult when you come to the end of a book. For months I have lived—and relived—my journey as a committed believer who struggled to live out his faith.

The wounds from your sin are real and can lead to death if you let them bleed out:

- *Healing and forgiveness are real.*
- *Wounds do become scars.*
- *Restoration is real.*

So for all those who fight for their faith and help others fight for theirs... For most of us, it is never as easy as we think it should be. We wrestle with doubts sometimes. We lose our focus at times. We even slide into the ditch sometimes. But we fight. We fight to be faithful to our calling. We fight to regain and maintain our focus. We fight our way back into the light. We fight against the temptations Satan uses against us. We fight.

We fight for—and with—others. As those committed to being spiritual helpers, we join together to do battle. We fight for those who are trying not to give up and just surrender to the enemy. We fight with those determined to return to the light. And stay there. We fight against the powers of sin and darkness in our world.

But our fight is not in some abstract denouncing of sin. We are committed to getting down into the mud and mire of the pigpen to help others get out. We wade into the battle where the blood flows to stop the bleeding and help the healing.

I do want to finish with a couple of personal notes—things that have made a difference in my life.

I have talked about developing plans for your spiritual recovery. I do think it is wise to have a strategy—plan to keep you focused. I have shared these with hundreds of church leaders over the years. I acknowledge these may not be for everyone, but they give an idea of what these plans might look like. Of course, yours will differ because it will be geared to your specific situation.

I want to highlight the reasons for these rules.

They protect you from temptation. It is always smart not to put yourself in harm's way.

They protect your flock as a church leader. They give those close to you confidence in your intention to be the person God wants you to be.

They protect you from false accusations. I always thought there were enough true things that nobody would make things up. But some people do. After all, you have a track record. There will always be some who assume the worst and will believe the worst.

So make your own rules, but these have helped me. And after a while, they even become second nature. ■

RIDGELL RULES

Why?

- I do not want to betray my Lord.
- I want my spouse and church to know I can be trusted.
- I do not want anyone to accuse me of something that is not true.

My Ten Commandments

- Do not counsel members of the opposite sex by yourself behind closed doors.
- Do not have extended conversations with the opposite sex unless someone is able to hear your side of the conversation.
- Do not have lunch alone with members of the opposite sex.
- Never travel alone with a member of the opposite sex.
- Always be sure someone knows where you are and what you are doing.
- When communicating with members of the opposite sex, use "we," not "I."
- Keep no secrets from your spouse. Be sure to share every password: emails and social media pages, and phones.
- Get accountability partners who can ask the hard questions. When in doubt about a situation, ask one of your partners.
- If someone makes you nervous, tell one of your partners.
- If one of your partners warns you, listen and act on it.

My Promise

- Follow the rules.
- Ask the hard questions.

It Is Well With My Soul

It is my favorite song. Ever. I have sung it all my life. It has been sung at our parents' funerals. The back story for this song is fascinating, but that is not the reason I love this song. I love it because the words speak to me.

And every time I sing it, or listen to it, I cry. Every time. Every single time.

I love the first verse because I do believe that "whatever my lot," I have been taught to say "it is well."

But it is the "sin" verse where I start to cry. I guess I should admit here that I am a world-class crier about Jesus. Singing. Preaching. Crying. But what Jesus has done for me is just so overwhelming and so undeserved.

"My sin—not in part but the whole, is nailed to the cross and I bear it no more. Praise the Lord." And I just teared up writing this. Best news ever.

Which is why the last verse matters.

"Lord haste the day when the faith shall be sight.

"It is well with my soul."

Wounds into Scars

I pray this book has helped and provided you with tools for the faith fighter.

The goal is for those bleeding from their sin wounds to be healed, for those wounds to become scars.

To help others on the journey to forgiveness and restoration.

So to all the faith fighters, God give you strength for the battle until by His grace, we all get home. ■

CPSIA information can be obtained
at www.ICGtesting.com
Printed in the USA
LVHW011242150922
728300LV00003B/9